Securing the Covenant

Securing the Covenant

United States–Israel Relations After the Cold War

Bernard Reich

PRAEGER

Westport, Connecticut
London

The Library of Congress has cataloged the hardcover edition as follows:

Reich, Bernard.
    Securing the covenant : United States–Israel relations after the
Cold War / Bernard Reich.
        p.   cm. — (Contributions in political science, ISSN 0147–1066
; no. 351)
    Includes bibliographical references and index.
    ISBN 0–313–29540–9 (alk. paper)
    1. United States—Foreign relations—Israel. 2. Israel—Foreign
relations—United States. I. Title. II. Series.
JX1428.I75R45   1995
327.7305694'09'049—dc20   94–37881

British Library Cataloguing in Publication Data is available.

A hardcover edition of *Securing the Covenant* is available from
Greenwood Press, an imprint of Greenwood Publishing Group, Inc.
(Contributions in Political Science, Number 351; ISBN 0–313–29540–9).

Library of Congress Catalog Card Number: 94–37881
ISBN: 0–275–95121–9 (pbk.)

First published in 1995

Praeger Publishers, 88 Post Road West, Westport, CT 06881
An imprint of Greenwood Publishing Group, Inc.

Printed in the United States of America

∞™

The paper used in this book complies with the
Permanent Paper Standard issued by the National
Information Standards Organization (Z39.48–1984).

10 9 8 7 6 5 4 3 2 1

Contents

Preface

For decades, as Israel has struggled to survive we have rejoiced in your triumphs and shared in your agonies. In the years since Israel was founded, Americans of every faith have admired and supported you. . . . In times of war and times of peace, every President of the United States since Harry Truman, and every Congress, has understood the importance of Israel. The survival of Israel is important not only to our interests, but to every single value we hold dear as a people. . . . I am committed to working with our Congress to maintain the current levels of military and economic assistance. We have taken concrete steps to strengthen Israel's qualitative edge. . . . As we help to overcome the risks of peace, we also are helping to build a peace that will bring with it the safety and security Israel deserves.
> —President Bill Clinton in an address to the Israeli Knesset,
> October 27, 1994

Israel is a special case in international relations. Although far away from the major world centers and comprising a small proportion of the world's territory and a small segment of its population, Israel elicits a high level of interest and receives a disproportionate amount of attention. Its actions are carefully scrutinized and analyzed for both their obvious and hidden meanings and for their long-term effects. Because Israel is an open society with a vigorous and free press and with substantial possibilities for debating the national interest and other matters, there is little about it that is not the subject of controversy. The

task for those concerned with United States–Israel relations has not been
to generate interest and to sustain it, as, for example, with U.S. policy
toward Africa, but rather to determine the nature and content of the
policy that will secure U.S. objectives.

The United States and Israel have been linked in a "special" relationship that existed prior to the establishment of the Jewish state in 1948
and has focused on the continuing U.S. support for the survival, security,
and well-being of Israel as an independent state in the Middle East. Israel
and the United States each occupy special positions in the other's foreign
policy, which are more than the sum of the tangible factors that can be
readily enumerated. The special relationship is marked by a continuity
and vitality that has fascinated observers but, nonetheless, has been the
subject of substantial discussion and controversy and has been marked
by misunderstanding, mistrust, and misconceptions.

This book is designed to reassess the foundations of the bilateral
relationship and to offer suggestions for its future in light of the end of
the Cold War, the Persian Gulf War, and the Madrid-inaugurated Arab-
Israeli peace process, especially the Israel-Palestine Liberation Organization Declaration of Principles of September 1993 and the Washington
Declaration of July 1994.

This study derives from my long-standing interest in U.S. Middle East
policy and in Israel's foreign policy. Its primary purpose is to describe
and to elucidate policy and to analyze rationales, as well as to suggest
possible future avenues of development and policies that might be
appropriate to consider. The work is organized thematically. It delves
into the background and evolution of the relationship between the two
states in the period since Israel's independence (1948), with appropriate
references to the pre-independence period.

This is not a diplomatic history designed to record all events in the
relationship, although much of the evolution can be identified in the
chronology appended to the work and many of the events are referred to
in the text as examples; rather, it seeks to provide a description and an
analysis of both United States and Israeli policy and the interaction of the
two states in the various arenas of the evolving relationship. It uses the
conceptual framework of a special relationship, and analyzes the
ideological, moral, political, strategic, and economic sectors of these
relations, as well as the U.S. political factor that has played a crucial role
in guiding the linkage. The formulation of policy in the United States is
not discussed in detail, although there are considerations of the political
component of the relationship focusing on the special ways in which
Israel is the subject of policymaking attention within the United States.

Although contemporary political analysis is always made more difficult by the nonavailability of secret government papers, there is also a wealth of sources that make this gap a minor one. The volume is based on research in official source materials in the United States and Israel as well as other primary sources and on interviews and discussions held over a period of more than three decades in both states (and elsewhere) with many of the policy makers and decision makers and others in positions of responsibility or with substantial knowledge of the course of events. The interviews have included cabinet members, government officials, general staff officers, congressional and parliamentary representatives, government experts, journalists, and scholars. I have also had access to unpublished papers and documents of various organizations and think tanks, and to U.S. and Israeli government unpublished materials, all of which have facilitated the analysis contained in this work. This book has also benefitted from my contact over the past decades with the unique Washington rumor mill and U.S. government agencies and from numerous visits in Israel and the Arab world and long sojourns there. Howard Rosen's chapter on the economic factor is similarly informed.

This study was concluded in the spring of 1994 as Israel and the Palestine Liberation Organization were in the process of implementing their Declaration of Principles and as the leaders of Jordan and Syria were contemplating the future course of their relations with Israel and with the United States. This preface was written as the Washington Declaration was issued by Jordan and Israel.

Acknowledgments

This volume owes its genesis to Richard Murphy, ambassador and former assistant secretary of state, who first talked me into the project and then established a series of seminars, in New York and Washington, under the auspices of the Council on Foreign Relations, during which the ideas and some of the words written here were first presented. In those seminars a number of individuals closely connected with the relationship, and some analysts and critics of it, suggested ideas that have found their way into my and Howard Rosen's thinking and analysis and some into the text of this volume. In addition, a number of U.S., Israeli, and Arab officials and academic colleagues have been kind enough to review some or all of the manuscript and have offered numerous suggestions for its improvement. Among those who participated in the seminars and/or who reviewed the draft were Graeme Bannerman, Raghida Dergham, Thomas Dine, Mark Erickson, Marvin Feuerwerger, Stanley Fischer, Leslie Gelb, Joseph Goldberg, Stephen Gotowicki, Peter Grose, John Hall, Rita Hauser, Arthur Hertzberg, Malcolm Hoenlein, Gershon Kieval, Judith Kipper, Khalil Jahshan, Les Janka, Bernard Lewis, Samuel Lewis, Richard McCormack, Judith Miller, Joseph Pelzman, James Prince, Samuel Sislen, Herbert Stein, Howard Stoffer, Peter Tarnoff, David Wurmser, Dov Zakheim, and James Zogby. Each deserves our thanks for their efforts to improve this work.

At the request of the Council on Foreign Relations I am including the following acknowledgment: "Research for this book was partly funded by a generous grant from the John D. and Catherine T. MacArthur

Foundation, which also made possible a series of seminars of the same topic at the Council on Foreign Relations, under the chairmanship of Hodding Carter III." Support for this work was also provided by the deans of Columbian College and by my successor as chairman of the Department of Political Science at George Washington University.

As before, Mim Vasan was especially understanding and helpful as the godmother of this work, while Ellen Dorosh was extremely cooperative in lending her considerable skills to the editing and production of this book. David Salzberg assisted in the construction of the index. The book is dedicated to Suzie who has long been involved in all aspects of the study of this subject and, as always, facilitated both the research and writing of this work.

Securing the Covenant

1

The Special Relationship

We have deepened and strengthened our relationship to the point where it is probably the closest that we have with any of our friends and allies anywhere in the world . . . We support Israel because it is our major democratic ally with strategic and ideological and cultural ties that grow stronger each year . . . As we work to achieve the goal of peace in the Middle East, we are guided by the fundamental principle which forms the basis for the peace process: our absolute commitment to Israel's security and to close U.S.-Israel relations. . . . The security of Israel is important to us, and we make no bones about it. . . . The U.S. stands by Israel in an unshakable partnership for peace.

— Vice President Al Gore,
"U.S. Middle East Policy: A New Era of Cooperation,"
35th Annual AIPAC Policy Conference,
Washington, DC, March 13, 1994

The relationship between the United States and Israel is a special relationship for special reasons. It is based upon shared interests, shared values, and a shared commitment to democracy, pluralism and respect for the individual.

— Secretary of State Warren Christopher, February 1993

A NEW BEGINNING?

The momentous event — the signing of the Israel-Palestine Liberation Organization (PLO) Declaration of Principles (DOP) — celebrated on the White House lawn in Washington, D.C., on September 13, 1993, ushered in a new era in the politics of the Middle East and altered, forever and irreversibly, the nature of the Arab-Israeli conflict and of all those other factors so inextricably linked to that conflict, including the United States' special relationship with Israel.

The signing of the DOP by Israeli Foreign Minister Shimon Peres and PLO Executive Committee Member Mahmoud Abbas in the presence of PLO Chairman Yasser Arafat and Israeli Prime Minister Yitzhak Rabin and witnessed by Andrei Kozyrev, foreign minister of the Russian Federation, and Warren Christopher, secretary of state of the United States, was followed by the famous handshake of Arafat and Rabin, encouraged by President Bill Clinton. The symbolism of that event and the euphoric mood it created over-shadowed the difficulties in implementing and expanding the documents that were to follow. Clearly caught up in that mood, observers and pundits began to expound on the significance of the event and to draw conclusions that suggested an optimistic, if not euphoric, picture of the region developing in a short time. Predictably, the optimism of the moment soon gave way to the reality of what remained to be done, not only in implementing the terms of the immediate accord but also in extending the process to those items that had been deferred for future negotiation and agreement and the expansion of the negotiation process to include the other negotiating partners with which Israel had engaged since the Madrid Peace Conference of 1991.

It was clear that the Middle East had been altered, as demonstrated by this unpredicted conviviality of two long-time adversaries and their U.S. supporters, but exactly how and in what ways remained unclear. Within weeks, some of the obstacles to future progress became obvious. Delays in implementation and vocal opposition within both the Israeli body politic and the Palestinian camp, in the occupied territories and beyond, soon marked the process. The process was soon overshadowed by what became known as the Hebron massacre in late February 1994.

The importance of the United States' role in assuring the continuity of the process became more obvious. At the same time it suggested elements of both continuity and change in the special relationship with Israel. Clearly implementation of the process would involve a series of decisions and actions that would, over time, test the covenant between the United States and Israel and the various components of their ties to each other. Throughout the postsigning period there were the usual consultations between the United States and Israel to reassess the changing situation and to coordinate an effective approach to the DOP, the broader peace process, and the U.S.-Israel relationship.

DEFINING THE SPECIAL RELATIONSHIP

The United States and Israel are joined in an unparalleled, complex, and multifaceted special relationship. Aimed at assuring Israel's survival, security, and well being, this special relationship rests on ideological, emotional, and moral pillars and on a commitment to democratic principles buttressed by strategic and political factors. Although all bilateral relationships are unique, the U.S.-Israel relationship is special. It is singular in nature, possesses exceptional attributes, and deviates from the norm in U.S. foreign relations in a positive manner.

In his "Iron Curtain" speech of March 5, 1946, Winston Churchill described the special relationship between the United States and Britain as one characterized by friendship and mutual understanding. U.S. and British policymakers, representing kindred societies and drawing on a shared political inheritance, enjoyed intimate relations. If they had "faith in each other's purpose, hope in each other's future, and charity towards each other's shortcomings," the United States and Britain could work together as friends and partners on common tasks of high purpose "that are dear to us and bode no ill to any." Churchill's description might well apply to the special relationship that later developed between the United States and Israel.

The U.S.-Israel relationship is an active partnership. Similar social systems and extensive individual ties link the two countries. Shared ideals and values sustain a strong psychological bond between the American and Israeli peoples, as do parallel, if not always congruent, political and economic interests. The relationship has endured over decades, surviving numerous crises and evolving over time from a more or less traditional one into the special relationship of today.

The special relationship goes beyond that of military alliances that are built solely on a common hostility to another party and often are marriages of convenience (for example, the anti-Iraq Gulf War coalition of 1990–91) of quite dissimilar parties that would not otherwise have much in common (for example, the United States and Syria). Some of the unique aspects of the U.S.-Israel relationship developed early (such as the shared values), but others, such as the strategic connection, came only later.

Despite the positive character of their links, perfect congruence of perspective and policy between the two partners is rare. Although the relations are special, points of discord and difficulty exist from time to time; but these are not permanently damaging and there is a rapid recovery and a return to close ties. The U.S.-Israel relationship is replete with examples of this oscillation. Endurance and resilience are trademarks of this special relationship, the hallmark of which is the ability to endure crises in which the parties have conflicting interests. There often are periods of coolness and discord on specific issues, but because of the relationship's fundamentals the United States and Israel come together again for mutual advantage. In this sense, the United States and Israel have a familial linkage — it is intimate and intense, and each is involved in the affairs of the other. Israeli envoys enjoy privileged access to the president and other senior U.S. officials, just as Israel's government regularly welcomes U.S. diplomats and numerous visiting dignitaries. Israelis have exploited their access to the Congress and their connections with the U.S. Jewish community to influence the nature and direction of U.S. policy and can identify a measure of achievement in that effort. At the same time, they have avoided becoming entangled in U.S. elections and partisan struggles even though, at times, Israelis have preferred one or another party or candidate. For its part, the United States has sought, also with some success, to affect the outcome of Israel's elections and the direction of its policies.

Americans have an intense interest in developments in and concerning the Jewish state, leading to extensive and detailed media coverage. This interest can be measured by the extent to which public opinion polls inquire about the partner state, the extent to which newspaper editorials and letters to the editor or the media focus on it, and the amount of time allotted on television and radio news programs.

The special relationship can also be seen in the laudatory public statements of U.S. officials as well as in the preferential treatment Israel receives from Washington, especially compared to other regional states. The United States and Israel often vote alike in the United Nations and other international bodies, and Israel's voting pattern on major issues often has the highest correspondence of any United Nations member with the voting of the United States. Israel was the first country to have a free trade area with the United States. (The fact that U.S.-Israel trade is modest only partly accounts for its having been established with less difficulty and controversy than the North American free trade area.)

Special preferences exist in all areas of interaction, including defense (both the quantity and quality of military assistance), economics (in trade and aid), science and technology, cultural exchange, and diplomatic support (for example, United Nations vetoes). (See Tables 1.1, 1.2, and 1.3.)

Candidates for public office in the United States give Israel disproportionate and positive attention in their position papers and campaign rhetoric. The platforms adopted quadrennially by the major U.S. political parties single out Israel. For example, the 1992 Democratic Party platform noted: "The end of the Cold War does not alter America's deep interest in our longstanding special relationship with Israel, based on shared values, a mutual commitment to democracy, and a strategic alliance that benefits both nations." The Republican Party platform acknowledged "Israel's demonstrated strategic importance to the United States, as our most reliable and capable ally in this part of the world . . . [and] the only true democracy in the Middle East." Israelis have similarly acknowledged the singularity and significance of the relationship with the United States, even while recognizing areas of disagreement. In presenting his government to the Knesset in July 1992, Prime Minister Yitzhak Rabin noted: "Sharing with us in the making of peace will also be the United States, whose friendship and special closeness we prize. We shall spare no effort to strengthen and improve the special relationship we have with the one power in the world."[1]

Although other states have attained a particular significance, none (with the exception of Great Britain and, to an extent, Canada) has achieved the status, over an extended period, of the special position accorded to Israel by U.S. popular opinion and reaffirmed by successive administrations and Congresses. Recognition of the interest and of a pro-Israeli bias and emotional commitment is widespread and generally accepted, even by those who question the wisdom of it.

The U.S. commitment to Israel is rooted in strong Biblical and historical emotions and ideology galvanized by feelings of guilt and obligation arising from the Holocaust. The return of the Jews to their homeland is unprecedented, unique, and warranting of international and especially U.S. support. Israel is seen as a like-image state whose survival is crucial to the ideological future of the United States.

Shared values and shared ideals that encompass the emotional, ideological, and moral connections between the two states undergird the commitment to Israel. The underlying element is democracy, complemented by a common interest in a stable, peaceful, and more democratic Middle East in which Israel is accepted and recognized as a

TABLE 1.1
U.S. Assistance to Israel
              (FY1949–FY1993, millions of dollars)

Year	Total	Year	Total
1949	100.0	1972	480.9
1950	—	1973	492.8
1951	35.1	1974	2,646.3
1952	86.4	1975	803.0
1953	73.6	1976	2,362.7
1954	74.7	TQ	292.5
1955	52.7	1977	1,787.5
1956	50.8	1978	1,822.6
1957	40.9	1979	4,913.0
1958	85.4	1980	2,146.0
1959	53.3	1981	2,408.4
1960	56.2	1982	2,245.5
1961	77.9	1983	2,500.6
1962	93.4	1984	2,626.6
1963	87.9	1985	3,371.7
1964	37.0	1986	3,658.5
1965	65.1	1987	3,035.2
1966	126.8	1988	3,034.9
1967	23.7	1989	3,039.9
1968	106.5	1990	3,428.0
1969	160.3	1991	3,705.1
1970	93.6	1992	3,091.0
1971	634.3	1993	5,090.0
		TOTAL	61,198.3

Notes:
   — = None
   TQ = Transition Quarter (U.S. fiscal year changed from June to September)
Source: Clyde R. Mark, "Israel: U.S. Foreign Assistance," *CRS Issue Brief*,
Congressional Research Service, The Library of Congress, updated February 24, 1994,
p. 13.

TABLE 1.2
U.S. Military Assistance to Israel
            (FY1949–FY1993, millions of dollars)

Year	Loan	Grant	Year	Loan	Grant
1949	—	—	1972	300.0	—
1950	—	—	1973	307.5	—
1951	—	—	1974	982.7	1500.0
1952	—	—	1975	200.0	100.0
1953	—	—	1976	750.0	750.0
1954	—	—	TQ	100.0	100.0
1955	—	—	1977	500.0	500.0
1956	—	—	1978	500.0	500.0
1957	—	—	1979	2,700.0	1,300.0
1958	—	—	1980	500.0	500.0
1959	0.4	—	1981	900.0	500.0
1960	0.5	—	1982	850.0	550.0
1961	*	—	1983	950.0	750.0
1962	13.2	—	1984	850.0	850.0
1963	13.3	—	1985	—	1,400.0
1964	—	—	1986	—	1,722.6
1965	12.9	—	1987	—	1,800.0
1966	90.0	—	1988	—	1,800.0
1967	7.0	—	1989	—	1,800.0
1968	25.0	—	1990	—	1,792.3
1969	85.0	—	1991	—	1,800.0
1970	30.0	—	1992	—	1,800.0
1971	545.0	—	1993	—	1,800.0
			TOTAL	11,212.5	23,614.9

Notes:
    — = None
    * = less than $100,000
    TQ = Transition Quarter (U.S. fiscal year changed from June to September)

Source: Clyde R. Mark, "Israel: U.S. Foreign Assistance," *CRS Issue Brief*,
Congressional Research Service, The Library of Congress, updated February 24, 1994,
p. 13.

TABLE 1.3
U.S. Economic Assistance to Israel
              (FY1949 - FY1993, millions of dollars)

Year	Loan	Grant	Year	Loan	Grant
1949	—	—	1972	—	50.0
1950	—	—	1973	—	50.0
1951	—	0.1	1974	—	50.0
1952	—	63.7	1975	—	344.5
1953	—	73.6	1976	225.0	475.0
1954	—	54.0	TQ	25.0	50.0
1955	20.0	21.5	1977	245.0	490.0
1956	10.0	14.0	1978	260.0	525.0
1957	10.0	16.8	1979	260.0	525.0
1958	15.0	9.0	1980	260.0	525.0
1959	10.0	9.2	1981	—	764.0
1960	15.0	8.9	1982	—	806.0
1961	16.0	8.5	1983	—	785.0
1962	45.0	0.4	1984	—	910.0
1963	45.0	—	1985	—	1,950.0
1964	20.0	—	1986	—	1,898.4
1965	20.0	—	1987	—	1,200.0
1966	10.0	—	1988	—	1,200.0
1967	5.5	—	1989	—	1,200.0
1968	—	—	1990	—	1,194.8
1969	—	—	1991	—	1,850.0
1970	—	—	1992	—	1,200.0
1971	—	—	1993	—	1,200.0
			TOTAL	1,516.5	19,522.4

Notes:
 — = None
 TQ = Transition Quarter (U.S. fiscal year changed from June to September)

Source: Clyde R. Mark, "Israel: U.S. Foreign Assistance," *CRS Issue Brief*, Congressional Research Service, The Library of Congress, updated February 24, 1994, p. 13.

legitimate state. The ideological-emotional bond is of long duration, but, despite its historical antecedents in the early days of the American experience, it was after the Six Day War of 1967 that it achieved its key position in the American mind.

The abiding interest in the survival of Israel has been articulated by every U.S. administration since 1948 and is a logical derivative of the proposition that the supreme interest of the United States is the preservation of its democratic way of life within a larger community of democratic nations.

Americans have traditionally been sympathetic toward peoples striving for nationhood and independence and toward persecuted peoples in particular, which inclined them to look with favor on the aspirations of Jewish nationalism. The Zionist claims received a wide hearing because of the presence of millions of Jews in the United States, and encountered greater receptivity because of their association with the Bible and its prophecies. Special sympathy also emerged because of the Holocaust. Support for Israel derived from a guilt complex but also served as a means to make amends for a terrible tragedy; a Jewish state provided a welcome place of refuge for the survivors. Truman and others clearly saw the need to support the creation of Israel in part as a reaction to the guilt factor resulting from the Holocaust and the extermination of 6 million Jews by Nazi Germany. Truman saw an opportunity to make some restitution for this barbaric act. There is also a feeling of moral responsibility for the preservation of Israel because of the United States effort that helped to establish the state. Truman identified a moral responsibility to honor an obligation, derived from the Balfour Declaration, that focused on the establishment of a Jewish state in Palestine.

Israel's special place in U.S. thinking antedates its emergence as a state. Manifestations of support for the aspirations of the Jewish people to return to Zion can be traced to President John Adams. Woodrow Wilson believed that this not only involved the "rebirth of the Jewish people" but also the potential for new ideals and ethical values for mankind that would spring from having the Jews restored to their land. Wilson endorsed the Balfour Declaration of 1917, as did Congress, individual senators and congressmen, and numerous state governments and legislatures. Such support was no doubt rooted in the influence of the Old Testament on the Founding Fathers and the spiritual legacy they provided to succeeding generations. The Hebrew scriptures served as guidelines for the lifestyle of the Puritans and other early pioneers and were subsequently embodied in the fabric of American life. The

Christian American religious heritage helps to secure a link to the land and people of Israel; there is a bond between the Christians of the United States and the Jews of Israel derived from the original Pilgrims who came to America from Europe to escape religious or political persecution. Religious faith later became a factor in support for Israel in the American Christian, and especially fundamentalist, communities. Hebrew was a major language of study in U.S. colleges and universities in their early days and there was a religious and spiritual connection with the Land of the Bible and its Jewish (not Arab) inhabitants. U.S. political leaders identified a religious component in their decision making. Truman saw the Jews deriving a legitimate historical right to Palestine from the Old Testament and would cite Biblical verses to support that view. Lyndon Johnson told B'nai B'rith in September 1968: "Most, if not all of you, have very deep ties with the land and with the people of Israel, as I do, for my Christian faith sprang from yours. The Bible stories are woven into my childhood memories as the gallant struggle of modern Jews to be free of persecution is also woven into our souls."[2]

Jimmy Carter recalls,

In my affinity for Israel, I shared the sentiment of most other Southern Baptists. . . . The Judeo-Christian ethic and study of the Bible were bonds between Jews and Christians which had always been part of my life. I also believed very deeply that the Jews who had survived the Holocaust deserved their own nation, and that they had a right to live in peace among their neighbors. I considered this homeland for the Jews to be compatible with the teachings of the Bible, hence ordained by God. These moral and religious beliefs made my commitment to the security of Israel unshakable.[3]

The U.S. evangelical movement provides strong grassroots support for Israel. Fundamentalist Christians are deeply committed on religious grounds to the concept of a homeland for the Jews in their ancestral territory and to support for the state of Israel. Evangelical preachers, evangelists, theologians, publicists, and their adherents in churches and television audiences have a significant and keen, although overwhelmingly spiritual if not theological, interest in Israel. They see the fate of Israel linked to their own salvation, in part because it is to Israel that Christ will return to establish his Kingdom in Jerusalem. Israel is a fulfillment of Biblical prophecy — the Old and New Testaments predict the return of the Jews to the Holy Land and the creation of a Jewish state in Israel before the second coming of Christ. Some see Israel as the fulfillment of the promises of God to the Chosen People (that is, the

Jews) — thus the covenants of God with the Jewish people remain valid for the Israelis today.

There is a broad affinity between the United States and Israel, and there is in the United States a widespread goodwill toward Israel that favored the establishment and consolidation of a Jewish state in Palestine and its continued existence, integrity, and security. There is an element of cultural similarity that identifies Israel as a "Western" state among oriental entities and as a perpetuator of the Judeo-Christian heritage. Israel is perceived as sharing the concepts of individual freedom and as a free, open, and democratic society pursuing peace. Political figures and others have described Israel as a stable democracy; a modern, developed, brave, valiant, gallant, dynamic, pioneering, peace loving, scientifically-oriented, egalitarian, and spirited state, a trusted friend of the United States fighting for survival. Its people are praised for their sacrifice, courage, tenacity, mettle, industriousness, dedication, determination, and spirit. Despite its precarious existence, Israel has achieved substantial progress and is identified as a model worthy of emulation. Shared values, cultural affinities, a common ethical and religious heritage, the Judaic tradition, and the Judeo-Christian heritage bind the United States and Israel together.

Americans have felt a strong empathy for Israel as a democratic nation and a society imbued with the liberal values and humanistic culture of the West. Vice President Walter Mondale noted in 1978,

So long as America believes in its own professed ideals, there will *always* be a special relationship. . . . There is no country anywhere in the world which more accurately reflects our basic values — freedom of speech, of worship, of political participation, freedom of every individual to seek his or her own pursuits. It is this truth more than any other — the values that we hold in common — which accounts for the special relationship.[4]

Israel's democracy did not evolve from some authoritarian form of government, nor was it forced upon it; it is an inherently democratic state. The Zionist movement set the pattern for Israel's democratic concepts and institutions. Political parties, platforms, and processes of the Zionist movement and of the Jewish community in Palestine (*Yishuv*) during the British Mandate were democratic in nature. Israel is one of the small group of democracies that have emerged since World War II and continues to thrive. Israel has a parliament elected by free and secret ballot and a government that changes at the will of the governed by peaceful means and not by assassination or military action. Debates between and among political parties of different ideological persuasions and political attitudes are the norm of political life. These ideas are central in democratic Western political systems but are alien in the Middle East, where responsible and representative governments are not the norm. The United States has an interest in the survival of the relatively few democratic states already in existence. Israel is an exposed democracy. Many members of Congress and others see it as an extension of their own democratic ideology — it is a bastion of democracy in a sea of authoritarianism. The idea that democracies have a special place in U.S. foreign policy has been highlighted in political rhetoric throughout this century. Consistent with longstanding American tradition, Clinton stressed democratic values as a campaign theme. "Democracy has always been our nation's perfecting impulse," and "democracy abroad also protects our own concrete economic and security interests here at home."[5] Israel was among his examples of a "democratic ally." His argument rests on several elements:

Democratic countries do not go to war with one another. They don't sponsor terrorism, or threaten one another with weapons of mass destruction. Precisely because they are more likely to respect civil liberties, property rights, and the rule of law within their own borders, democracies provide the best foundations on which to build international order. Democracies make more reliable partners in diplomacy and trade, and in protecting the global environment.[6]

The professed concern with fundamental values includes support for human rights; pluralism; women's and minority rights; popular participation in government; and the rejection of extremism, oppression, and terrorism. These values are an important factor that distinguishes United States policy from that of most other states; this is the U.S. ideology and it is both an element and a goal of policy. The United States remains committed to encouraging greater openness and responsiveness of political systems throughout the world and can have truly close and enduring relations with those countries with which it shares fundamental values.

Like the United States, Israel is a nation of diverse immigrants who left inhospitable lands for a new one where they endeavored to build a just and free society. In the process they experimented with various forms of human association. The American experience in striving to escape persecution and establish an independent national homeland had a parallel in a Jewish state that appeared to reaffirm those ideals through absorption and integration of immigrants in distress. There is a corresponding dedication to the values of pioneering — the United

States placed a premium on the pioneers who heeded the call to "go west," and Israel placed a similar value on the settlers who moved to the frontiers to develop those areas.

Sympathy for Israel also derives from the American concern for the weak against the strong (the "underdog" sympathy factor) and the few against the many. This derived from Israel's underdog image relative to the Arab states during the first decades of the Arab-Israeli conflict, and has been attenuated somewhat in recent years.

These perceptions and shared values continue to undergird the U.S.-Israel relationship despite an evolution in how each element is perceived and forms a part of the whole. On June 24, 1992, then Assistant Secretary of State Edward Djerejian, described the linkage in these terms:

The U.S.-Israel relationship . . . is based on the firmest of foundations . . . shared democratic ideals and values; profound and extensive ties from the grass roots to the official level; and an unshakable U.S. commitment to Israel's security. U.S.-Israel relations in every sphere remain active and vibrant. . . . This does not mean — and has never meant — that the U.S. and Israel see eye to eye on every issue. . . . Our differences should not obscure . . . the fact that the U.S. and Israel share fundamental values and that we remain unshakably committed to Israel's security and to preserving Israel's qualitative edge over any likely combination of aggressors.[7]

2

The Partner

As the world's only Jewish state, Israel approaches all issues from a unique historical perspective. The State of Israel that formally came into being at the termination of the British Mandate in May 1948 was born of centuries of Jewish heritage and tradition that continue to affect all aspects of its national life. Israel recalls a Jewish history replete with episodes of persecution and clashes with outside forces seeking to overrun its homeland and to defeat and exile its people. The Jewish state emerged from an unparalleled confluence of forces in the nineteenth and twentieth centuries, including widespread anti-Semitism, the Holocaust, and two World Wars and their aftermaths.

Israel sees itself as having a number of interrelated missions: to preserve its independence and territorial integrity; to maintain its Jewish character (however imprecisely defined) and its links to Jews throughout the world; and to serve as a spiritual center, protector, and haven for Judaism's persecuted numbers. Israel's commitment to virtually unrestricted Jewish immigration is enshrined in its Declaration of Independence and the Law of Return and has been reinforced by successive governments, with overwhelming support in the Knesset and from its Jewish population. It has been implemented almost without regard to the economic costs and social dislocations caused by a rapid and massive population influx.

Despite Jewish-Zionist successes in gaining British government support for a "national home for the Jewish people" in Palestine, as expressed in the Balfour Declaration of 1917, no independent political unit was established after World War I; instead, Palestine was a British Mandate from 1922 to 1948. Although President Woodrow Wilson, and later the United States Congress, endorsed the Declaration, a lack of tangible British and U.S. support and practical developments jeopardized Zionist hopes. Clashes in Palestine between Arabs and Jews were commonplace during the Mandatory years, as each community sought to assert its position and to secure its claims to the territory after the British withdrawal. From the outset the Zionists and later the Israelis noted Arab opposition to the return of the Jewish people to the Land of Israel. This was seen as a rejection not only of the modern political Zionist movement, but also of the history and traditions of the Jewish people that focused on Zion — the Land of Israel.

The partition plan adopted by the United Nations General Assembly on November 29, 1947, divided Palestine between the Jews and the Arabs, and Jerusalem was placed under an international regime. Although this did not meet Zionist objectives, it was accepted by the Zionist leadership as the best attainable alternative. The Arab decision to reject the plan and to go to war against the nascent Jewish state was not merely a missed opportunity; it was a strategic decision by the Arab leadership that a Jewish state in any part of Palestine was unacceptable. The outcome was the Arab-Israeli conflict.

The first Arab-Israeli War (Israel's War of Independence) was followed by negotiations on the island of Rhodes that led to a series of armistice agreements in 1949. The refusal of the Arab states to negotiate for anything beyond the armistices set the tone for the ensuing period during which hostilities have continued and peace has remained elusive. The face presented to Israel was one of unremitting hostility.

THE CENTRALITY OF SECURITY

Israel's preeminent and overriding preoccupation with national survival and security derives from Israel's conflict with its Arab neighbors and its geostrategic location and dominates, directly or indirectly, all aspects of Israeli life. This has prevailed since 1948, when its declaration of independence was greeted by invading Arab armies dedicated to the destruction of the fledgling state. Israel has fought six major wars[1] (excluding the Iraqi Scud missile attacks in 1991 during the Gulf War) and, despite the ongoing peace process, has failed to establish peace with any of its Arab neighbors except Egypt and, now, Jordan. Countless skirmishes, terrorist attacks, and incessant, vituperative rhetoric against the state, which only now has been modified by some Arab sources, have reinforced Israel's perception of the danger it faces. As a consequence it spends a major portion of its state budget, GNP, and GDP on defense. It has a sizable standing army and even larger reserve force, although it views Arab hostility to be less menacing today than it was at independence and in the initial ensuing decades.[2]

The Arab position was codified and enshrined in the Khartoum Arab Summit formula adopted after Israel's victory in the Six Day War in 1967 — no peace with Israel, no recognition of Israel, no negotiations with it, and adherence to the rights of the Palestinian people in their country — and was illustrated in the broad opposition to the Sadat initiative, the Camp David Accords, and the Egypt-Israel Peace Treaty, as well as some applause for Saddam Hussein's anti-Israel rhetoric and Scud missile attacks during the Gulf War and opposition to the Israel-Palestine Liberation Organization (PLO) Declaration of Principles (DOP) signed in September 1993.

Israel's perception of the Arab threat was reinforced by its geographical isolation and compounded by the absence of formal alliances with other states committed to come to its defense or provide support in the event of war. No state has fought alongside Israel in its wars and none is obligated to do so in future hostilities. Although its position in the international system has varied, until the end of the Cold War it was generally treated as a pariah state and systematically excluded from the major caucuses and blocs in the United Nations and elsewhere. This situation has improved in recent years because of the restoration or establishment of diplomatic relations between Israel and the states of Eastern Europe, the former Soviet Union, Asia, and Africa.

Israel's geographical and political isolation was compounded by its geographical vulnerability. The frontiers that existed between the armistice agreements of 1949 and the Six Day War of 1967 were difficult to defend and were vulnerable to enemy attack, as were its population centers. The country was small, and there were no significant natural defense barriers. Lacking strategic depth, Israel's main military facilities were within enemy artillery range and within easy reach of hostile forces. These factors helped to shape Israel's view of the significance of the territories it occupied during the Six Day War and its postwar policy of not returning to what Abba Eban often referred to in his United Nations speeches as the "fragile and perilous" armistice lines. After 1967 the concept of defensible (or "secure") borders became central to Israel's military planning.

Israel viewed the threat to its security as regional in scope and, until the establishment of the Islamic revolutionary government in Iran, confined to the Arab world. In a narrow military sense, the greatest threat was posed by the confrontation Arab states — those that share a common frontier with Israel (Egypt, Syria, Jordan, Lebanon), plus Iraq. Later Israel included other Arab states in its definition of the threat because they provided vocal, political-diplomatic, financial, and, occasionally, military support to the confrontation states. These states allied themselves with the confrontation states in the Arab League and other institutions (such as the United Nations), participated in Arab summit decisions against Israel, joined in the chorus of anti-Israel rhetoric, and provided some of the wherewithal for and occasionally sent troops or other personnel to participate in the wars, terrorism, and other military and paramilitary actions directed against Israel. After 1973, Israel added Saudi Arabia to the list of its antagonists because of Saudi Arabia's willingness to use its oil reserves and production, its substantial earnings in petrodollars, its growing and increasingly sophisticated military capability, and its regional and international political weight in the Arab efforts against Israel, including the use of the "oil weapon" and participation in the Arab boycott of Israel.

THE ALTERED THREAT ENVIRONMENT

The onset of the 1990s marked an improvement in Israel's overall security position. The implosion and breakup of the Soviet Union, which led to an overall reduction in the flow of arms to the Arabs (despite some arms deals and weapons supplies from the former Soviet Union and from states of the former Soviet bloc) as well as diminished political and diplomatic support, was a crucial element. The peace process inaugurated by the 1991 Madrid Conference allowed Israel to begin direct, official, and public negotiations with Arab partners (Syria, Lebanon, Jordan, and the Palestinians). The secret negotiations with the PLO in Oslo, the signing of the DOP, and the subsequent negotiations elsewhere contributed significantly to this process. Overall, these developments altered the threat by suggesting the possibility of peace and the normalization of relations with, or at minimum, a reduced threat from, one or more of its adversaries. Despite these and other changes, however, many Israelis have yet to be wholly convinced that the Arabs have changed their fundamental attitudes and policies toward Israel or that they accept Israel as a legitimate state.

This overall improvement came about despite the Gulf War, which had serious ramifications for Israel's thinking about security and strategy. Although the Scud missile attacks launched by Iraq against Israel caused few casualties and limited destruction of property, they had broad economic and psychological effects, paralyzing Israel for weeks. Israel's nonresponse raised questions about its ability to deter future Arab attacks. The U.S. refusal to allow Israel to participate in the anti-Iraq coalition raised doubts about the United States' perception of Israel's strategic value and the U.S. commitment to Israel's security.

Israelis view the world with skepticism and suspicion and analyze with meticulous care the actions and policies of the Arab states as well as those of friends and supporters. They read and interpret symbols with diligence, searching for hidden meanings and nuances of change. Not all Israelis have been convinced that the accurate interpretation of the Arab world is the one symbolized by the initiative of Anwar Sadat and the continuation of the Madrid DOP-inaugurated process, rather than the rejectionism of Saddam Hussein and his cohorts. Some Israelis remain more impressed by the fact that Israel has fought six major wars against the Arabs and endured countless acts of terrorism, than by the rhetoric of Arab spokesmen. The "cold peace" with Egypt had mixed results: it raised expectations that have not been met, and so far only Jordan has followed Egypt's lead, although some others have moved in that direction. Even the Madrid process has not fully altered the perspective. Israelis have long sought assurances that their Arab neighbors accept Israel's legitimacy, and events such as the refusal to support the repeal of the United Nations "Zionism is racism" resolution cast doubts on Arab intentions.[3] The continuing Arab boycott, despite modifications, affects negatively Israel's economy and remains a symbol of Arab antipathy if not hostility.

The intifada (uprising) that began in the Gaza Strip and West Bank in December 1987, as well as the more recent activities of Hamas (the Islamic Resistance Movement), which combines Islamic extremism with calls for the destruction of Israel and the establishment of an Islamic state in all of Palestine from the Mediterranean Sea to the Jordan River, raised questions about the willingness of the Palestinians to negotiate even after the signing of the DOP. The Arab uprising in violent opposition to the continued Israeli occupation of those territories soon became a test of wills and policy between Palestinians in the territories and Israel. Israel's attempts to end the uprising damaged Israel's international image and affected Israel's psyche while it convinced some Israelis of the imperative of disgorging the territories. Others remained adamant that control of the territories cannot be granted to those who were engaged in violence against the Jewish state and its people. Nevertheless, there were changes wrought by negotiations and agreement in Oslo and enshrined in the DOP. Although the ultimate effect is not yet established clearly, there are and will be alterations in Israel's thinking.

The Gulf War's effects are more complex. Yasser Arafat and other Palestinians championed Saddam Hussein, whose antipathy to Israel was well known, arguing that his actions supported the Palestinian position, and Saddam Hussein sought to use the Palestinian cause to help rally support for his efforts against Iran and against Kuwait. (Iraq has remained technically at war with Israel since the first Arab-Israeli War, having refused to sign even an armistice agreement with the Jewish state). In the spring of 1990, the Iraqi leader threatened to "burn" half of Israel. After the invasion of Kuwait, he sought to link his control of that territory acquired through aggression with Israel's occupation of the West Bank and the Gaza Strip, despite the obvious dissimilarities between the two situations. His argument that the Scud attacks on civilian targets in Israel were in support of the Palestinian cause was a cover for the real motive: to break the coalition united against him. The image of Palestinians "cheering the Scuds from the rooftops" further confirmed Israeli doubts about the chances for real peace negotiations. In allying the PLO with an aggressor against whom much of the international community was aligned, Arafat raised doubts about his, and the PLO's, credibility. However the support for Saddam Hussein may have been justified within the Palestinian and Arab worlds, to many Israelis it reinforced the argument that Palestinians posed a threat to the existence of the Jewish state. Later, this view was modified, but not eliminated, by the Oslo talks' outcome.

On the other hand, the serious damage done to Iraq's offensive capability during the Gulf War has postponed the threat and clearly improved Israel's security position in the short term. The war also highlighted the significant division in the Arab world. Iraq's invasion of Kuwait and the emergence of Islamic political forces (commonly, but incorrectly, referred to as Islamic fundamentalism)[4] in Algeria and elsewhere forced the Arab states to reorient their relationships with each other. General Uri Sagy, the head of Israeli military intelligence, summarized Israel's threat assessment in an interview in *Yediot Aharonot* on April 17, 1992:

In light of the developments in the region since the Gulf War, I estimate that the immediate [i.e., for some months and perhaps extending for a year or two] conventional military threat facing the State of Israel has decreased. The main reasons for this are the military defeat of Iraq, the U.N. efforts to disarm it, the collapse of the Soviet Union as a meaningful strategic element in the region, and the United States' standing as the only prominent superpower.

Subsequent evaluations were similar in their scope and direction.

Nonetheless, Israelis were still worried about the long-term Arab threat. Syria continued to enhance its military power and to achieve an expanded order of battle by acquiring strategic and improved weapons systems, including chemical and perhaps biological weapons and precise, long-range, surface to surface missiles. Newly acquired advanced Scud C missiles give Syria the ability to use nonconventional warheads to hit any target in Israel from protected positions in its territory. Israel is concerned about Syrian purchases of sophisticated hardware and technology from China and North Korea and believes that Syria is cooperating with Iran in missile development. Anxiety about Iraq's nuclear capabilities lingers despite Israel's attack on the Osirak reactor in 1981 and the damage done to Iraq's facilities by the Gulf War in 1991. Although a special United Nations commission has sought to remove, render harmless, or eliminate Iraq's declared or known nuclear weapons materials and equipment, it is not clear that Iraq has lost its long-term nuclear weapons capability. Iraq may well have hidden parts of its program, valuable equipment, and perhaps even stocks of enriched uranium. In any event, it retains the technologies developed by the scientists, engineers, and technicians who worked on the program.

The Arab threat to Israel is compounded by Iran's political and military ambitions and its goal of becoming a regional superpower. In combination, Iran's size, wealth, resources, and relative freedom of activity compared to Iraq's, make it potentially a greater threat than prewar Iraq. Its growing military might must be factored into any equation concerning Israel's future strategic needs. There is widespread concern about Iran's efforts to develop a nuclear capability at the same time that it is acquiring a short and long range missile force and seeking chemical weapons. The ability of an unpredictable revolutionary Iran to threaten regional states was enhanced with the destruction of Iraq's military capability in the Gulf War and the resultant partial vacuum that Iran, motivated by Islamic and hegemonic inclinations, was eager to fill. Israel believes that Iran has the personnel and resources to develop nuclear weapons and worries about its close cooperation with other states in the attempt to produce long range surface to surface missiles in addition to possible cooperation in the nuclear sector. North Korea apparently has supplied Iran (and other regional states) with Scud C missiles and technology to develop longer range missiles.

Although the Iranian program is only the latest of these efforts to engender Israeli anxiety, the possibility that an Arab or Muslim country might develop a nuclear weapon (a so-called "Islamic bomb") has concerned Israel since the 1970s. Israeli officials worry that Iran has established links with a number of countries capable of providing technical aid and components for a nuclear weapons program, including China, North Korea, Pakistan, India, and several others in Western Europe. Israel's concerns about Iran's ambitions are exacerbated by Teheran's opposition to the Madrid peace process and by its efforts to establish closer links with the Central Asian Islamic republics of the former Soviet Union. Israel is also uneasy about the role that scientists and other weapons experts from the former Soviet Union might play in Iran's nuclear program, as well as in other military development and production efforts. Israel is concerned about Iran's conventional force buildup, which includes the acquisition of Scud missiles with increased range and the addition of the more than 100 Iraqi jet aircraft that had been flown to Iran during the Gulf War and were incorporated by Iran into its air force. Iran is known to be a major supporter of international terrorism and other subversive activities, giving aid to the Hezbollah in Lebanon as well as to Islamic extremists in the Sudan, Egypt, and Algeria. Iranian-inspired Islamic extremism has added to Israeli concerns not only because of its support for Hamas but also because of Iran's efforts to destabilize pro-Western regimes and because of attacks on U.S. interests.

Islam in its various local and regional political manifestations remains a matter of growing concern for Israel. Nevertheless, Islam is not the replacement for communism as a unifying threat in the Middle East on which a joint U.S.-Israel strategic relationship can be built.

THE SOVIET FACTOR

Although Israel was concerned about Soviet bloc actions during the Cold War, neither the Soviet Union nor the bloc states were central components of the perceived threat nor of Israel's strategic planning. The Soviet Union supported Israel's creation by voting for the partition plan of November 1947, accorded it *de jure* recognition shortly after independence, and endorsed its applications for membership in the United Nations. It provided moral, political, and material support to the new state during its War of Independence, and Czechoslovakia was an important source of arms and materiel.

Except for the early years, the Israeli-Soviet relationship was primarily adversarial, if not confrontational. Some incurable Israeli optimists (mostly in the Israeli Communist Party and MAPAM) remained convinced of the possibility of close links between Israel and the Soviet Union, especially in the first decade after Israel's independence, but they were not central in Israel's political and decision-making elites. Primarily, Israelis viewed the Soviet Union in a negative light, as the armorer of Israel's adversaries, as their "lawyer" who provided them with political and diplomatic support, and as the primary donor of economic and technical assistance to the Palestinians and the Arab states. Soviet political-diplomatic and military support for the Arab position was troublesome, especially when it included the provision of expert advisers, as well as limited participation in conflict, such as flying combat missions in the Suez Canal zone during the War of Attrition in the spring of 1970, but it was not at the core of Israel's security concerns, which focused on the threat posed by the Arab states. Israel acknowledged the potential of the Soviet threat, but it was seen as beyond Israel's capabilities. It was to be dealt with by the United States and the West. After the Egyptian-Czechoslovakian arms deal of September 1955 firmly established a foothold for the Soviet bloc as a major actor aligned with the Arabs and advocating their position, Israel's leadership sought to develop close relations with a major Western power to counter the Soviet role. Israel turned to France and the United States for arms supply and political and diplomatic support.

The Soviet role as patron and armorer of the Arab states has been significantly reduced, and this has altered the Arab ability to challenge the Jewish state militarily, forcing policy reassessments in the Arab world and consequently in Israel. In its waning years, as part of an overall modification of its domestic and foreign policies, the Soviet Union had already begun to shift away from providing arms to the Arab states. It also opened a dialogue with Israel and eventually reestablished diplomatic relations with it. It permitted the connection between Israel and Soviet Jews to flourish and allowed substantial Jewish emigration, despite strong Arab opposition and formal protests to Moscow. Between January 1990 and June 1994 more than 500,000 Jews of all age groups and professional skills emigrated from virtually all of the major republics and regions of the former Soviet Union to Israel, providing a boon to Israel by adding to its human capital and reaffirming the Zionist principles on which Israel was founded. In all of these changes the United States effort was important. Especially during the Reagan administration, U.S. policies proved instrumental in fostering a new Soviet approach concerning Israel and Soviet emigration.

For Israel, the end of the Soviet Union as an alternative superpower was far less momentous than for the radical Arab states who lost their patron, their armorer, and their advocate in the struggle with Israel.

Unlike the Arab states, moderates included, who lost the option to "play off" the United States against the Soviet Union, Israel never enjoyed this option and so lost little in the reconfiguration of the superpower balance.

With the end of the Cold War, the potential for involvement of the Soviet Union in Arab-Israeli hostilities and the possibility that this might lead to a military confrontation between the United States and the Soviet Union ended. The East-West overlay of the Arab-Israeli conflict disappeared and, with it, the Soviet threat to Israel. The successor states, especially Russia, increasingly have turned to playing a positive role in the Arab-Israeli peace process and to developing a normalized relationship with Israel.

SECURITY AND FOREIGN POLICY

Israel's response to its security threat was grounded from the beginning in the concept of self-reliance. Their awareness of the main events that constitute the drama of Jewish (including Israeli) history led Israelis to the conviction that the Jews (read also Israelis) could not depend on others. There must be a Jewish state to provide a refuge for Jews under duress and it must have a defense capability adequate to protect its citizens and ensure its survival and, by extension, the survival of the Jewish people. In order to counter the permanent asymmetries between Israel and the Arab states — its numerical inferiority and the territorial, resource, and financial disparities — Israel sought to achieve and sustain a qualitative edge over the combined power of its antagonists. To this end, Israel relies on highly trained and motivated personnel equipped with sophisticated and advanced weapons systems.

From the outset, even before the founding of the state, the Israel Defense Forces and its predecessor organizations worked to acquire the military means to counter the identified Arab threat. This, in turn, generated a continuous effort to secure military equipment in quantities to ensure the country's defense.

Israel's foreign policy began to take shape once it became clear that peace would not follow the armistice accords of 1949. Israel tried to reduce its political isolation by directing its attention beyond the circle of neighboring Arab states to the broader international community as well as trying to establish links with minorities in the Arab world. It worked to establish friendly bilateral relationships with the states of Europe and the developing nations of Africa, Asia, and Latin America, as well as with the superpowers. The centrality of the Arab-Israeli conflict enlarged and enhanced the role of the superpowers, particularly the United States.

Israel felt compelled to elicit the backing of at least one major European
power for weapons supply as well as for political and diplomatic support.

From the early 1950s until 1967, France filled this role as an unde-
clared ally of Israel, while the United States played a more limited part.
For France, there was the benefit of links with a state that was opposed to
Gamal Abdul Nasser's growing Arab world role and his strong anti-
colonialist posture directed against the European colonial powers
(England and France). The "tacit alliance" with France was more of a
marriage of convenience with mutual benefits derived by the participants than a full-fledged alliance, and its quality suffered after Algeria's
independence in 1962. After the Six Day War the United States became
the consequential external power whose role was, in part, to deter the
Soviet Union. But Israel continued to believe in self-reliance and to be
wary of dependence on others. It was ambivalent about alliances, as well
as skeptical of international or great power guarantees. De Gaulle's
abrupt alteration of the French-Israeli relationship in 1967, after more
than a decade of France's role as a reliable friend and ally, suggested to
Israelis that such linkages are fragile and could break with little warning.
These attitudes also derive from events associated with the Six Day War:
the sudden removal of the United Nations Emergency Force from the
Sinai Peninsula, the failure of the United Nations Secretary General to
intervene to prevent escalation of the tensions, the impotence of the
Security Council, and the inability of the United States to construct an
international naval flotilla to ensure freedom of passage in the Gulf of
Aqaba.

At independence some of Israel's political elite, including Foreign
Minister and later Prime Minister Moshe Sharett, argued for a policy of
neutrality or nonalignment in the Cold War and saw the potential for
support from both superpowers, despite a general proclivity toward the
West. The presence of a substantial Jewish population in the Soviet bloc
and their fate was a factor in these considerations. Nevertheless, in the
ideological struggle between the democratic and communist political and
social orders, Israel chose democracy. By 1950, Israel became linked
with the West, and its relationship with the Soviet Union and the Soviet
bloc deteriorated. Initially, Israel looked on the United Nations as a
benign and even positive actor, but eventually came to see the organization as little more than a forum for the articulation of Soviet and Arab
policy on Arab-Israeli issues. The end of the Cold War, and the success
of the effort against Iraq, suggested the possibility of an altered approach
by the United Nations that might allow it to play a more significant role
in Arab-Israeli issues. Movement in that direction marked the period

after the General Assembly voiced its "Zionism is racism" resolution and
the Madrid Conference reinaugurated the peace process.

As the foreign policy of Israel became Western oriented in the 1950s,
the United States' relationship with Israel remained proper, and sometimes even positive, but had not achieved the extensive and positive
levels that were to develop following the Six Day War. The West
provided Israel with political and moral support, arms, and economic
assistance essential for its survival and defense, while the Soviet Union
increasingly identified itself with the Arab cause. Ultimately, Israel's
relationship with the United States became the most significant. The two
states developed a diplomatic-political relationship that focused on the
resolution of the Arab-Israeli conflict. The United States committed
itself to terminating the conflict and thereby assuring Israel's peaceful
existence in the Middle East. Periodically it initiated programs to achieve
that objective, but these were all unsuccessful. No significant arms
supply or economic assistance was provided. The relationship moved
into a new phase and became especially close after the Six Day War
when a congruence of policy prevailed on many of their salient concerns,
although the two states often held differing perspectives of regional
developments and of the dangers and opportunities they presented. No
major ruptures took place despite significant tensions at various
junctures. At the same time, an exclusivity developed as six major Arab
states broke diplomatic relations with the United States after the
hostilities.

Although it developed ties with a number of European states, such as
France, Holland, and Germany as well as the European Community,
Israel's multifaceted relationship with the United States has been the
major exception to its go-it-alone posture. Despite the substantial links
that have developed between the two countries and the widespread belief
that the United States is committed to Israel's security, the exact nature
of the United States commitment to Israel remains imprecise. There is no
formal alliance.

Israel's elite has not been uniform in its views of the United States and
the role it plays in support of Israel. There has been an ambivalence
concerning United States support. The United States remains Israel's
"best friend" and most important and dependable supporter. Nevertheless
its reliability has varied and is not a wholly firm foundation for the development of Israeli policies. As each new instance of United States support
is welcomed, there is a tinge of concern voiced at different times from
different elements of the political spectrum, conditioned by prior

experiences. Israelis are concerned about the wider world in which the bilateral relationship is conducted.

On the positive side, the United States has provided Israel with economic, technical, military, political, diplomatic, and moral support, and has been central to the Arab-Israeli peace process. During the Cold War the United States was the ultimate resource against the Soviet Union in the region. The positive support included the resupply, albeit with delays, during the Yom Kippur War, the extensive history of generosity in aid and related areas, support in the United Nations for Israel's position even when that meant they stood alone against the remainder of the international community, and the use of the veto in the Security Council to sustain Israel's position or to shield it from hostile actions.

On the negative side, Israelis have sometimes seen the U.S. role as less than wholly supportive and reliable — it has been ambiguous and often its policies have been at odds with those of Israel on specific aspects of the Arab-Israeli conflict.

During Israel's War of Independence, the United States did not send forces to the endangered new state nor did it take any other meaningful steps, such as arms supply, as the United States adhered to its 1947 arms embargo even when British arms were available to the Arabs. There was an indifference to the fate of the Jewish community in Palestine and the Truman administration's policies were not wholly favorable. In the spring of 1948, the United States proposed a temporary suspension of the partition plan and sought a special session of the United Nations General Assembly to consider a potential trusteeship for Palestine. The arms embargo put into effect in December 1947 severely limited arms supply to the fledgling state, and none came from the United States. Economic aid was limited and no significant U.S. effort to resolve the Arab-Israeli conflict was launched in these early years. Other incidents also raised questions about the sincerity and commitment of the United States.

The Eisenhower-Dulles tenure was viewed in a more negative light, as exemplified by an unwillingness to make a formal commitment to Israel's security and its refusal to balance the Czechoslovakian-Egyptian arms deal of 1955 by providing Israel with U.S. arms. Only after significant delay did the United States suggest that its allies provide the weapons Israel needed. The 1956 Suez crisis and war led to serious tensions in the relationship, and the Arabs have continually cited that period as the one they wish emulated in United States policy. The United States opposed the tripartite collusion (Israel, Great Britain, and France) and supported United Nations efforts to terminate the conflict. Crucially, United States pressure on Israel forced it to withdraw from the Sinai

Peninsula without any serious moves toward peace. Overall the relationship was often cool in the 1950s.

Israeli disappointments continued in the 1960s as the Kennedy administration launched intensive efforts to woo Egyptian President Gamal Abdul Nasser and others such as King Hussein of Jordan and the leaders of Iraq, Saudi Arabia, and Lebanon, as well as because of specific policy initiatives. United States statements and actions in the Security Council and elsewhere on cross border raids, responses, and regional tensions also raised questions about the solidity of its policy and support for Israel. The United States did not use its Security Council veto to shield Israel from Arab and Soviet efforts to undermine its legitimacy through condemnatory United Nations resolutions. There was a disappointing lack of action by Washington before the Six Day War in support of its pledge to maintain Israel's freedom of passage through the Strait of Tiran that was made by John Foster Dulles on behalf of the U.S. government in February 1957.

The Rogers plans (1969–70), named after Richard Nixon's Secretary of State, caused great consternation. Israel's cabinet formally rejected the proposals on the grounds that they prejudiced the chances of establishing peace, disregarded the need to establish secure borders through peace treaties arrived at by direct negotiations, and affected Israel's sovereign rights when it proposed resolutions concerning refugees and the status of Jerusalem. Similarly the two power and four power talks in 1969 and 1970 that focused on a settlement of the Arab-Israeli conflict generated Israeli anxiety because they were discussions concerning Israel's future about which Israel knew little and there were few and limited communications between the United States and Israel.

Relations between the United States and Israel were generally friendly when Henry Kissinger served as Secretary of State, but there were moments of consternation. There was forced resupply of the encircled Egyptian Third Army at the end of the Yom Kippur War. Kissinger suggested that the United States would provide supplies if Israel did not allow Egypt to do so. Clearly his view was that this was essential to prevent the surrender of the Third Army and the humiliation of Anwar Sadat, which would have undermined Kissinger's view of the postwar conditions needed to move toward an Arab-Israeli settlement. Israel agreed to the relief procedure only after substantial U.S. pressure. In 1975 there was the reassessment of U.S. Middle East policy that was widely seen as an effort to blame Israel for the failure of the Kissinger shuttle to achieve an accord between Israel and Egypt. Examples of Israeli concern about U.S. reliability were identified in the Carter and

Reagan years as well. For example, the United States-Soviet Union joint communique of October 1977 raised the specter of the superpowers seeking to impose their version of a solution to the Arab-Israeli conflict on the parties. In 1982 the Reagan "fresh start" initiative was undertaken without adequate consultation with Israel.

In the wake of the Gulf War, some Israeli defense analysts suggested Israelis were not convinced of the actions the United States might take if Saddam Hussein had sent his forces toward Israel rather than into Kuwait. Israelis were unconvinced that the United Nations Security Council would have been as responsive and doubted that the United States would have succeeded in mobilizing an international military coalition to come to Israel's aid.

THE "NEW" ISRAEL AND ITS VIEW
OF THE UNITED STATES

When the Labor Party emerged from the June 1992 Knesset election as the largest party and Yitzhak Rabin moved quickly to form a new government, an initial wave of euphoria swept many in Israel as well as external observers (especially in the United States). In Israel, the left of center and others in the "peace camp" believed that this would facilitate the peace process and improve the prospects for a negotiation process with the Arabs that might lead to agreements to resolve aspects of the Arab-Israeli conflict. Similarly, in the United States officials who had long toiled on the peace process and pundits, and others critical of Shamir and Likud and the reluctance of the right-wing government to make concessions, were elated and hopeful that the peacemaking process would be invigorated and that U.S.-Israel tensions evident in the confrontations between the Bush administration and the Shamir government would be eased.

The central themes of the policy agenda remained the same, despite obvious changes in decision makers and in ideology as well as in performance. Israel's perception of the threat and thus of the consequent role of the United States was characterized by some, albeit limited, differences. Rabin, reflecting the pragmatism of the professional military officer, saw opportunities in the changed political and international environment created by the demise of the Soviet Union and by the defeat of Iraq. The collapse of the Soviet Union and its ability to play a significant role in the Middle East altered the threat to Israel's security, although the possibility that the former republics might continue to sell arms to the Arab states (and Iran) arrayed against Israel was still a cause for concern.

After his election Rabin sought to ease the tensions between Shamir's government and Bush's administration through moderate and conciliatory rather than confrontational speeches and other statements and interviews, through his manner and improved atmospherics, and through changed domestic and foreign policy priorities and actions on such issues as settlement construction, reduced government spending in the occupied territories, the early release of some Palestinian prisoners, and the cancellation of the planned expulsion of some Palestinians from the occupied territories.

From the outset, the Bush administration's relationship with Israel was less positive than that that had prevailed during the Reagan tenure. Differences before the Gulf War on issues such as settlement construction and the role of the Palestinians in the peace process were exacerbated afterward when the United States pressed for movement on an Arab-Israeli peace process. Israel was not convinced that the Arab world was ready to move toward peace, and the pressures on Israel to participate were not always accompanied by the pledges and reassurances that, in the past, have often persuaded it to negotiate despite skepticism concerning the motives of its interlocutors. This was compounded by the high profile public clash of the Bush administration with the Israeli government and the pro-Israel lobby in the fall of 1991 on housing loan guarantees (see below).

Israel, concerned with both procedure and substance, approached the Madrid peace conference in 1991 with trepidation. The United States was determined to convene a conference and was less troubled by Israel's objections. Israel was, however, successful in imposing conditions in exchange for its participation, especially concerning the Palestinian role. Substantive differences between the United States and Israel focused on the interpretation of United Nations Security Council Resolution 242 — although they agreed that the resolution did not require Israel's total withdrawal from the occupied territories (which the legislative history supports), they disagreed on the extent of withdrawal and whether it was required on all fronts (the Sinai Peninsula, the Golan Heights, the West Bank, and the Gaza Strip). Israel rejected the concept of insubstantial alterations, articulated by then Secretary of State William Rogers to refer to minor changes in the 1967 frontiers between Israel and the West Bank and Gaza Strip, because it did not comport well with Israel's conception of required adjustments. The immediate problem, however, revolved around Israel's establishment of settlements in the occupied territories (which in the United States' view included East Jerusalem) that Israel saw as a legitimate right of Jews in the Land of Israel and that the Bush administration condemned as both illegal and an obstacle to peace.

The complexities of the U.S.-Israel relationship and the peace process became apparent again in early January 1992, as the United States joined in a United Nations Security Council resolution condemning Israel for deporting Palestinian activists to Lebanon after a series of Palestinian terrorist acts against Israelis in the occupied territories and in Israel proper. Israel read the action as a modification of U.S. policy that raised doubts about the role that the United States might play in the peace process.

Israel has never been willing to relinquish the right to decide for itself what actions are essential to ensure its survival and security. Also, in the past, Israel sought an activist U.S. role in the Middle East as a counterweight to Soviet machinations. This view was held both by groups that emphasized the Soviet role and danger and those that tended to minimize it. Those that saw a strategic Soviet role in the region hoped that, especially if they called attention to it, the United States would be alert and would contain it, counter it, and provide Israel with the ultimate defense against it. With the demise of the Soviet Union and its challenge dissipated, the United States is no longer needed to balance the threat and challenge posed by the Soviet Union.

Israelis recognize that the United States must play a role in initiating and facilitating a peace process to resolve the conflict and gain Israel's acceptance in the region.[5] However, this does not mean that the process proposed by the United States or the content of its policies on specific elements of the dispute will be those necessarily preferred by Israel. In any event, Israel sees the United States as the facilitator, not the maker, of peace. Israelis continue to see peacemaking as a function of the parties to the conflict rather than the domain of the international community or the remaining superpower.

Ultimately, Israel's conception of the threats to its security and survival, and the siege mentality, will determine its willingness and ability to move forward toward a comprehensive peace. Its domestic political situation and its ability to make peace will be affected by its feeling of security and the translation of that fear, or the lack of it, into political support for the government and its peacemaking efforts.

When Yitzhak Rabin became Prime Minister in the summer of 1992, he sought to move Israelis to a new perspective by appealing to them to abandon the garrison outlook that had shaped and governed much of their history. He argued that that mentality was no longer a valid framework for thinking about peace and security, as had been argued by Menachem Begin and Yitzhak Shamir in their rhetoric and world views. This perspective was challenged toward the end of 1992 and the first months of 1993, as Hamas initiated a series of violent acts in the occupied territories and Israel in an effort to derail the peace process. Rabin began to refer to Hamas as a terrorist organization, accusing it of murdering innocent Israelis in order to prevent any movement toward peace. In December 1992, he deported more than 400 Islamic fundamentalists from the territories. Later he closed off the West Bank and Gaza Strip, preventing Palestinians from travelling freely into Israel. These actions reinforced Israeli fears of Islamic extremism.

Israelis welcomed the Israel-PLO DOP, but continue to be skeptical of international security guarantees. Although they recognize and appreciate the contributions made by the United States to their survival and security, many Israelis tend to see this as a function of the United States acting in its own interests. Israel's long-held view that it does not seek U.S. troops to assure its security has been further amplified in the post–Cold War period. Israel continues to see its security assured by its own forces and not by outside powers, including the United States. While Israel seeks military and economic assistance as tangible expressions of the U.S. commitment, it has been particularly adamant about its long held policy of self-reliance. It does not want U.S. troops fighting in or for Israel. The dangers inherent in such participation have been recognized and this judgment appears validated by U.S. experiences in overseas military involvements. Vietnam-analogous situations cause great discomfort in Israel's decision-making circles. The exceptional instance of U.S. soldiers operating Patriot missile batteries in Israel during the Gulf War has not altered the doctrine of self reliance.

The United States will continue to be central, if not indispensable, to Israel in the future as it has been in the past. Despite the essential character of the relationship, Israelis do not delude themselves concerning the serious questions that remain as points of actual or potential discord between themselves and the United States — including the nature and extent of future strategic cooperation and the United States commitment to maintaining Israel's qualitative edge over its Arab and Iranian adversaries. Israelis suspect that the end of the Cold War and the experiences of the Gulf War may have altered the special relationship with the United States in irreversible ways. With the Soviet threat now a memory and the United States focusing inward, there is a concern that Israel may be increasingly dismissed as just another country of five million people. However, the United States remains essential to Israel as a source of economic and military assistance and of intelligence that it cannot acquire through its own sources and methods. U.S. electronic and satellite capabilities would supplement that which Israel has and can deploy to acquire essential information. Arms supply remains the main area of U.S. strategic support. Israel cannot produce on its own the weapons it requires — evidence the Lavi jet fighter program — to maintain its qualitative edge.

How will United States relations with Israel's adversaries affect the special relationship? How should Israel deal with the fact that the United States has a growing relationship with the Gulf Arab oil producing states? Israel is concerned that the growing militarization of the Gulf Cooperation Council and of Iran poses a serious challenge, especially when the United States is the primary armorer of the Gulf Cooperation Council. Will the United States continue to sustain Israel's qualitative edge, and what will be the cost to Israel of this arms race? The role of the United States is likely to become problematic as it increasingly becomes a military supplier to the Arab world because of its perception that the Arabs require sophisticated arms for their own security, and that it is in the best interests of the United States to supply such arms not least because arms sales are important for the United States economy. It also has been argued that this will work to Israel's advantage, because otherwise the Arab states would have to enter the broader international arms market, where the United States could not impose restrictions on types or qualities of weapons or limitations on their use. As long as these friendly Arab states are intent on weapons purchases, the argument goes, it is to Israel's advantage that the United States be the provisioner, because this will gain influence for the United States and enhance Israel's security. Israel has not accepted the logic of this argument and the pro-Israel lobby in the United States has overwhelmingly opposed it. The United States thus will increasingly find itself in the position of providing equipment to the Arab states and of then having to compensate Israel to assure its qualitative edge. The dilemma is, of course, for the United States to make decisions while taking into account competing rationales for United States military supply. For Israel to oppose United States arms sales to the Arab states is increasingly likely to prove futile. Arms sales clearly affect the regional military balance, but opposition to such sales runs into the hard facts of economic necessity in the United States. Thus, Israel will need to focus its efforts on security compensatory arms supply to sustain its qualitative edge.

The decision by President Bush to sell 72 F-15 aircraft to Saudi Arabia in 1992 is a case in point. Prime Minister Rabin objected to the sale because it would negatively affect Israel's security, but he understood that despite Israel's opposition the sale would go forward for economic reasons, so he sought to avoid provoking a political controversy. Thus, Israel lodged a pro forma protest with the United States and concentrated on securing pledged compensation in order to strengthen its own capabilities in the development and production of essential defense equipment. In addition to U.S. aid for its defense industries, Israel bargained with Washington for enhanced strategic cooperation, the prepositioning of advanced military equipment in Israel, the transfer of military equipment, including helicopters and sensitive technology, to Israel, and the sharing of satellite intelligence.

Despite some concerns about the United States as a wholly reliable partner, Israel still views the United States as the essential element in ensuring its survival and security, in maintaining its strategic qualitative edge, and in potentially guaranteeing a peace agreement with its Arab neighbors. The special relationship, with all its flaws, remains essential to Israel's survival and security.

The Israel-PLO DOP illustrates this point. Although the negotiations were conducted in secrecy and Norway played the crucial role of host and facilitator, the signing ceremony on September 13, 1993, took place in Washington, as did the Donors Conference designed to secure the funds to implement the first phases of the agreement. Once again this demonstrated the centrality of the United States in the peace process. It was only the United States that could secure the famous handshake between Rabin and Arafat and play the crucial role of sustaining the momentum of the process thereafter, despite numerous challenges to it. For the PLO and the Arab states, the United States' special relationship with Israel gave the United States a role that could not be usurped by any other state, because only the United States could secure the required actions from Israel. For Israel the combination of United States involvement in the process and the reassuring of Israel that its security and well-being would be sustained made the continuation of the process possible. Clearly an Israel ready to move toward peace could only be a country reassured by the special relationship with the United States that provided its ultimate guarantee of security as it made concessions for peace.

3

The Strategic Connection

The strategic connection of the special relationship involves the issue of Israel's strategic value to the United States, Israel's survival and security, and arms acquisition and the military balance.

THE STRATEGIC CONTEXT

In the superpower rivalry and competition that characterized the international system from the end of World War II until the end of the Cold War, the Middle East was a principal focus of national security and foreign policy attention and provided a framework for United States relations with the regional states.

As it planned for the organization of the international system after World War II, the United States did not see a significant role for itself in the Middle East. The prevailing assumption was that the region would continue to be of more consequence for its allies, particularly Great Britain and France, and there was no anticipation of a Soviet threat to the region that might engender a U.S. response. However, the rivalry for hegemony in the Middle East began soon after the end of World War II, with the Soviet-supported challenges to postwar regimes in Greece, Turkey, and Iran. Responding to Soviet political-military challenges and seeking to prevent Soviet hegemony or even spheres of influence in the region became a tenet of U.S. policy and encouraged the initial United States involvement in the northern tier states, the promulgation of the Truman Doctrine, and the U.S. aid program for Iran. When the Soviet

Union later expanded its activities in the Arab-Israeli and Persian Gulf sectors, the United States obsession with these machinations led to a determination to counter these moves. These responses were codified in policy doctrines such as those of Eisenhower (1957) and Carter (1980) designed for the Middle East and those of Nixon and Reagan that had significant applications in the region. These approaches saw the dominant threat to the Middle East as Soviet-Communist in nature and framed its policy accordingly.

U.S. interests in the Middle East included a commitment to Israel's survival, the need to assure U.S. and friendly state access to the region's oil and its markets, and the desire to sustain positive relationships with moderate Arab states. Resolution of the Arab-Israeli conflict was essential because it impinged on all the other interests. That conflict threatened regional stability and the survival and security of Israel, generated Arab oil embargoes, and raised the specter of a superpower clash arising out of their competition for regional influence.

The issues faced by U.S. policy in the Arab-Israeli sector of the Middle East were different from those elsewhere in the region — they were not Soviet generated and the consequent policy responses took an alternative form. In the immediate aftermath of World War II, the United States assumed responsibility for the displaced persons (primarily Jews) liberated from German concentration camps. This policy was based on the plight of the Jews in Europe — a humanitarian rather than a strategic consideration. For those Jews who had survived the Holocaust and wished to do so, Truman saw immigration to Palestine as an appropriate solution to their humanitarian problems.

Only in 1947 with the British decision to relinquish the Mandate and withdraw from Palestine did the United States face a political-strategic issue, and even then the strategic considerations were not dominant. Truman's decision to support the creation of a Jewish state was not motivated by Israel's strategic value to the United States, nor was he dissuaded by the argument that it was a strategic liability. Truman took the decision to support the United Nations partition plan and the consequent creation of a Jewish State in Palestine (Israel) primarily for humanitarian reasons. The pleas of Zionist leader and, later, Israeli President Chaim Weizmann had impressed him, and he also considered the domestic U.S. political factor (that is, the American Jewish vote). Those in his administration, such as Secretary of Defense James Forrestal, who were focused on strategic considerations advised Truman that the oil resources and the size of the Arab world were of greater significance to the United States than an independent Jewish state. They argued that U.S. support of a Jewish state would be a strategic liability, that there would be significant and irreparable damage to U.S. interests (especially in the oil sector) in the Middle East and the Muslim world, and that there would be "worldwide repercussions." Clark Clifford, a Truman adviser, believed there was a strategic element in Truman's decision because if the United States had not supported Israel, its position would have been even more precarious in the ensuing Arab-Israeli war (known in Israel as the War of Independence). In that event, the United States might have faced a far more difficult decision about whether it should offer U.S. military support to the Israelis or risk watching the Arabs drive the Israelis into the sea.

A close strategic connection did not follow the creation of Israel; the developing relationship was rooted in ideological-emotional factors. Some in the defense community, especially the U.S. Navy, identified Arab oil as essential and wanted to safeguard its supply to the United States, but this viewpoint was not widely accepted and the United States was not to be meaningfully dependent on Middle East oil for several decades. Washington was primarily interested in preventing the Soviet Union from establishing control in the Middle East, which it viewed as a serious threat to United States access to the region's strategic lines of communication (such as the Suez Canal) and its oil resources. After Israel's independence there were strong pressures on President Truman to avoid a policy that included Israel and to resist Israel's requests for economic and military aid. The United States developed a policy that relied on the Arab states to confront the Soviet Union and Israel generally was not included. The proposal for a Middle East Defense Command (1951) saw Egypt as the centerpiece, with Israel excluded. The Baghdad Pact (1955) and the Eisenhower Doctrine (1957) were also Arab focused.

Although the United States was the first country to recognize Israel, the strategic connection was a limited one — the United States provided virtually no aid during Israel's War of Independence or in the years immediately following. Some military equipment was sold earlier, but the Kennedy administration inaugurated the first significant weapons sales with HAWK anti-aircraft missiles in 1962.

The Six Day War was an important watershed in the relationship. During the hostilities the United States provided tangential support for Israel but did not play a direct role — it did not engage in combat, nor did it resupply Israel, but it did move the Sixth Fleet to counter a potential Soviet intervention and supported Israel's position in the United Nations by opposing Soviet initiatives there. In the diplomatic round that followed the hostilities, the United States provided strong political and diplomatic support and took the initiative in shaping the postwar situation. Lyndon Johnson's June 19, 1967 speech enunciating principles for peace in the Middle East established a framework for postwar diplomacy.

Restraint continued to characterize U.S.-Israel relations in the strategic realm even after Israel's substantial victory over its Arab foes. They did not establish a true strategic connection, although there were increasing instances of arms supply to Israel and statements endorsing Israel's survival and security. At the same time, the United States was a deterrent to Soviet direct involvement in combat and it foiled Soviet diplomatic initiatives, although it did not counter or fully match Soviet military supply to its Arab clients with comparable equipment for Israel. Israel, in turn, contributed to the burgeoning strategic connection. Its positions in the Sinai Peninsula and along the Suez Canal prevented the Soviet Union from using the canal to shorten its supply lines to the Indian Ocean and Southeast Asia. Israel also provided the United States with valuable military intelligence and information about captured Soviet equipment that facilitated United States countermeasures against similar weaponry in Vietnam. Israeli experience with United States equipment in combat led to modifications in design and tactics against Soviet bloc armaments. Nonetheless, Israel did not consider the United States to be a strategic ally in the formal sense, nor did the United States regard Israel as a strategic asset.

In 1970, the United States faced a new reality: a deteriorating regional situation linked to the presence of large numbers of Soviet advisers in Egypt, including pilots who were flying operational missions and other personnel who were operating Egypt's missile defense system. President Richard Nixon compared the region to the Balkans in 1914 and worried about a war breaking out in the Middle East that might involve the superpowers. National Security Adviser Henry Kissinger spoke of expelling the Soviets from Egypt; indeed their preoccupation with the region formed the basis for the convergence of U.S. and Israeli interests. Nixon declared U.S. support for the maintenance of the regional balance of power and for Israel's deterrent strength in order to discourage the Arabs from launching another war that might lead to superpower confrontation.

Israel proved its value to the U.S. and to King Hussein in the Jordan crisis of 1970. By reinforcing its own forces on the Golan Heights, it deterred Syrian intervention in support of the Palestinians fighting King Hussein. Israel acted at Washington's behest and the Nixon administration expressed its appreciation for Israel's cooperation. This was the genesis of the view propounded by some in the administration and others, such as Senator Henry Jackson in the Congress, that Israel served United States strategic interests in the Middle East, that it could become a factor in the protection of the moderate Arab regimes, and that it could be a bulwark against the spread of Soviet influence.

During the 1973 Yom Kippur War the United States provided Israel with crucial arms and ammunition during the hostilities but again did not participate in combat. Kissinger's goal, however, was to prevent a decisive Israeli military victory that would humiliate Egyptian President Anwar Sadat and the Arabs, as in 1967, and thereby to facilitate armistice and, later, peace negotiations. Before the onset of hostilities, Kissinger believed that it was imperative that Israel not launch a preemptive strike and he warned against such an action. Prime Minister Golda Meir decided "for political reasons" that Israel would not do so, despite strong pressure from Israel's decision-making elite. After the Egyptian and Syrian attacks, she asked Washington to resupply Israel with equipment and ammunition. The United States took the unprecedented step of airlifting supplies to Israel during the fighting. The stalemate at the end of the hostilities facilitated the process that led to Israel's disengagement agreements with Egypt and Syria in 1974, as well as to the Sinai II Accords in 1975. The 1975 agreement and the accompanying memoranda with their commitments and pledges on matters such as oil supply, economic and military assistance, and the peace process consolidated the existing strategic connection.

Despite the Camp David Accords and the Egypt-Israel Peace Treaty, the U.S.-Israel strategic connection was not greatly expanded in the Carter administration. Nevertheless, Jimmy Carter wrote in his memoirs: "For the well-being of my own country, I wanted the Middle East region stable and at peace; I did not want to see Soviet influence expanded in the area. In its ability to help accomplish these purposes, Israel was a strategic asset to the United States."[1] Despite these sentiments, Israel's dependence on the United States for arms increased but its role as an ally was not enhanced.

With the fall of the Shah of Iran in January 1979, Israel lost a guaranteed source (if not always at a reasonable price) of oil, as well as a sometime friend and supporter on some aspects of the Arab-Israeli conflict. The Islamic Republic of Iran soon established close links with the Palestine Liberation Organization (PLO) and other radical elements in the Arab world and supported their hard line positions against Israel. The Carter administration's inability to "save" the Shah also raised concerns in Israel and other regional states such as Saudi Arabia, voiced by government officials and analysts, about the reliability of the United States as an ally. American Jewish supporters of Israel also raised questions of this ilk. The Soviet invasion of Afghanistan in 1979 presented Washington with new problems in the Persian Gulf and Southwest Asia. The Carter Doctrine made it clear that the United States would use military force, if necessary, to protect its interests there. It was obvious that neither the fall of the Shah nor the invasion of Afghanistan were connected to the Arab-Israeli problem. To the contrary, Israel's position as a stable and reliable democratic state with a powerful military in a region of instability stood in sharp contrast to these developments.

Overt strategic cooperation between the United States and Israel developed in the Reagan administration as instability and insecurity became commonplace in the Gulf and Southwest Asia with the ousting of the Shah, the establishment of the Islamic Republic of Iran, the War in Afghanistan, and the Iran-Iraq War. Ronald Reagan had made public his own view of the special relationship before taking office. In an article published in the *Washington Post* of August 15, 1979, he argued:

American policy-makers downgrade Israel's geopolitical importance as a stabilizing force, as a deterrent to radical hegemony and as a military offset to the Soviet Union. The fall of Iran has increased Israel's value as perhaps the only remaining strategic asset in the region on which the United States can truly rely; other pro-Western states in the region, especially Saudi Arabia and the smaller Gulf kingdoms, are weak and vulnerable.

He identified Israel as "a major strategic asset to America. Israel is not a client, but a very reliable friend." President Reagan's ideas often coincided with those of the Begin government in Israel, although they were not usually shared by the professional levels in the Department of Defense, who could not readily identify specific roles for Israel in potential allied military operations in the Middle East.

The Reagan administration introduced the concept of "strategic consensus" that called for the regional states, from Pakistan to Egypt, to cooperate with Washington and among themselves in opposing a common Soviet threat. The challenge for the administration was how to convince these regional states that their primary security threat came in fact from the Soviet Union rather than from the other regional states. Strategic consensus required access and a regional network of support facilities for United States military forces, and Washington offered to increase arms sales to cooperating countries.

Israel embraced the strategic consensus initiative. The Reagan administration formalized and institutionalized, for the first time, certain military, economic, and political aspects of the U.S.-Israel strategic relationship. On November 30, 1981, Secretary of Defense Caspar Weinberger and Israel's Minister of Defense Ariel Sharon signed a Memorandum of Understanding (MOU) on strategic cooperation "designed against the threat to peace and security of the region caused by the Soviet Union or Soviet-controlled forces from outside the region introduced into the region."[2] The MOU was not directed at any state in the region, was limited in scope, and did not provide for joint military exercises, nor did it create a formal means of cooperation. For Israel, its significance lay in the fact that the United States identified Israel as a strategic partner rather than as a mere client or beneficiary, and that it held out the prospects of increased weapons transfers based on the perceived Soviet threat. The MOU signaled an improved relationship with Washington and mitigated some of the negative effects of the United States sale of Airborne Warning and Control Systems (AWACS) and other advanced weapons systems to Saudi Arabia.

However, the positive atmosphere resulting from the accord was soon dissipated when Israel, invoking historical and security factors as well as the refusal of Syria to recognize its existence and to negotiate for peace, extended its law, jurisdiction, and administration to the Golan Heights in December 1981. The United States quickly made it clear that it opposed any unilateral change in the status of the Golan Heights and it supported a United Nations resolution condemning Israel's action. It also suspended the MOU. Israel was stunned by the U.S. response. Prime Minister Menachem Begin made his unhappiness plain to Samuel Lewis, the U.S. ambassador to Israel. On December 20, Begin told Lewis that he regarded the suspension of the MOU as its cancellation. He went on to query whether Israel was a "vassal," a "banana republic," or a "fourteen-year-old boy" who was being punished for misbehaving. He added that the United States was not "morally" entitled to "preach" to Israel about some of its other recent actions such as the bombing of the Iraqi nuclear reactor, because of U.S. actions in World War II and Vietnam. Israel's invasion of Lebanon in June 1982 led to a further deterioration of the relationship. The Israeli military action against the PLO in Lebanon came suddenly. Within a week Israeli forces had destroyed or captured numerous PLO strongholds and were in control of much of the southern half of the country. By the middle of June, Israel had virtually laid siege to Beirut. The official U.S. position was that it did not collude with Israel and did not welcome the invasion, nor did it condemn it. U.S.

Ambassador Phillip Habib was instrumental in terminating hostilities between Israel and the PLO, the lifting of the siege of Beirut, arranging cease-fires, and negotiating for and arranging the withdrawal of the PLO from Beirut. U.S. troops, as part of a multinational force, arrived in Lebanon in late August to facilitate the PLO evacuation and were withdrawn in September after it was completed. U.S. and Israeli policies often clashed during these efforts. U.S. forces returned to Lebanon after the massacres of Palestinians by Lebanese Phalangists at the Sabra and Shatilla refugee camps, drawing the United States further into the Lebanese quagmire.

The war in Lebanon and the altered situation in the Israel-Lebanon-Syria sector that resulted created, in Reagan's view, the opportunity for an effort to achieve an Arab-Israeli settlement. Therefore, on September 1, 1982, the United States launched the Reagan "fresh start" initiative. Israel was not consulted in advance and saw the initiative as detrimental to its interests because it departed from the conceptual framework of Camp David and seemed to determine the outcome of negotiations on the status of Jerusalem and the future of the West Bank and Gaza Strip. These and other concerns led Israel to reject the proposals. The rejection, coupled with the Sabra and Shatilla massacres by the Phalangist militias, resulted in a decline in Israel's standing in American (as well as American Jewish) public opinion and further rancorous disagreements with the Reagan administration. By the summer of 1983, however, the U.S.-Israel relationship had reverted to positive levels. The Kahan Commission Report (in which Israel accepted some of the blame for the massacres), the failure of King Hussein of Jordan to join the peace process, the increased Soviet involvement in Syria, and the signing of the U.S.-promoted Lebanon-Israel agreement of May 17, 1983, coupled with the Syrian-Soviet opposition to it, all contributed to a significant improvement in Israel's standing in American public opinion (both that of the Jewish community and the public at large) as well as a warming of official relations. The U.S. involvement in Lebanon also contributed to an improved relationship. The United States sought to rebuild Lebanon as an independent sovereign state and attempted to accomplish this by reinforcing the government of Amin Gemayel (who succeeded his assassinated brother as President of Lebanon in September 1982), reconstructing Lebanon's economic infrastructure, nurturing a Lebanese army that would support the legitimate government, and achieving the withdrawal of all foreign forces. Israel's objectives in Lebanon generally coincided with Washington's. The failure of the Shultz-brokered May 17, 1983 agreement, due to opposition from Syria and the PLO as well as leftist and Muslim factions in Lebanon, led to improved relations and closer coordination between the two governments. Meanwhile, the major issues of discord between Washington and Jerusalem, which centered on the West Bank and Gaza Strip and the Reagan fresh start initiative, were not addressed in any meaningful way.

On October 29, 1983, Reagan signed National Security Decision Directive 111, which reinstated the concept of strategic collaboration with Israel and provided a basis for the development of a formalized structure of strategic cooperation. This opened the way for discussions on joint military exercises, the stockpiling of U.S. military equipment, the sharing of intelligence data, the use of Israeli ports by the Sixth fleet, and joint planning for possible military contingencies. This direction, like the 1981 MOU, emphasized the defensive nature of such cooperation and the fact that it was directed against the threat posed by the Soviet Union and its surrogates in the region, not against Israel's Arab neighbors.

When Prime Minister Yitzhak Shamir visited Washington in November 1983, the United States and Israel agreed as an outgrowth of the MOU to establish a Joint Political Military Group (JPMG) that would convene every six months as an official forum for discussions of military issues. Reagan pledged that the JPMG "will give priority attention to the threat to our mutual interest posed by increased Soviet involvement in the Middle East. Among the specific areas to be considered are combined planning, joint exercises, and requirements for prepositioning of U.S. equipment in Israel."[3] The JPMG held its first meeting in January 1984 and has met twice a year since then to review progress in the strategic arena. In the ensuing years strategic cooperation between the two countries increased: vessels from the Sixth Fleet have made port calls at Haifa, the United States leased Kfir jets from Israel, the two navies conducted joint antisubmarine warfare maneuvers, and the United States Air Force practiced bombing in the Negev.

More agreements followed. In late 1984 Secretary of Defense Caspar Weinberger and Defense Minister Rabin signed an agreement permitting Israel to compete directly in the U.S. market and to encourage sales of Israeli military equipment in and to the United States. In February 1985, Israel, in response to a message from President Reagan detailing his personal interest in and endorsement of the project, agreed to permit the building of a Voice of America relay station in the Negev.[4] In April 1985, Israel accepted Weinberger's invitation to participate in the Strategic Defense Initiative. Among the administration's considerations was that Israel's participation might help moderate Congressional opposition to the program. Israel in turn stood to benefit from technological spin-offs and from research and development contracts as well as from closer military links with the United States.

Then, on December 14, 1987, Defense Minister Rabin and Secretary of Defense Frank Carlucci signed a ten year memorandum of understanding that codified the rules for the military commerce between the two countries and gave Israel expanded opportunity to secure Pentagon contracts. Previously, Israel was permitted to bid only in specifically identified areas; under the new accord, Israel could bid on any Pentagon contract from which it was not specifically barred. Israel thus achieved the status enjoyed only by North Atlantic Treaty Organization (NATO) countries and two major non-NATO allies (Sweden and Australia), and it was designated a "major non-NATO ally."

In April 1988, on the fortieth anniversary of Israel's independence, the United States and Israel signed another memorandum of understanding. The White House noted that "the memorandum of agreement reiterates for the public record our longstanding relationship of strategic cooperation with Israel. It reflects the enduring U.S. commitment to Israel's security. That commitment will never flag. The President knows that a strong Israel is necessary if peace is to be possible."[5] Two months later, on June 29, 1988, the United States and Israel signed a memorandum of understanding to develop and produce jointly a new defensive missile, the Israeli Arrow, designed to intercept and destroy tactical ballistic missiles. The United States agreed to pay 80 percent of the research costs.

In the 1980s, Israel increasingly came to be viewed as a strategic asset and the only reliable ally of the United States in the Middle East by Ronald Reagan, other policymakers as well as congressmen, and other public officials. U.S. economic and military assistance had risen to $3 billion annually, all of it in grants, and was supplemented by millions more from special arrangements. Strategic cooperation became the catch-phrase of those who argued that Israel could be useful in supporting U.S. interests throughout the Middle East, including the Persian Gulf and the Arabian Peninsula. Nevertheless, many U.S. policymakers and strategic planners saw this as impractical, recognizing few circumstances in which Israel's participation would be invited or even welcomed. Some believed that Israel was a limited and perhaps flawed asset, as demonstrated by the decision not to use its facilities for the evacuation of wounded marines after the Beirut massacre, by the idea of creating a Jordanian, not Israeli, rapid deployment force for regional contingencies, and by efforts to build facilities for prepositioning U.S.

military equipment at Ras Banas in Egypt rather than use Israeli facilities.

By the end of Reagan's second term there were numerous areas of military cooperation that went beyond those spelled out in the formal memorandums of understanding. The United States Navy and Air Force were using Israel's live-fire ranges for training exercises. U.S. and Israeli forces were engaging in joint air and sea exercises, and the United States Navy was making extensive use of Israel's ports. Also, the United States and Israel had drawn up joint plans, for the first time, for responding to possible Soviet threats to their security interests. They were also cooperating on a variety of weapons development and production projects including aircraft, mini-RPVs (remotely piloted vehicles), electronics, naval vessels, tank guns, and terminal guidance bombs. A web of cooperative arrangements was in place that greatly facilitated defense trade between the two countries. Finally, a U.S. declaratory policy that openly embraced Israel as an "ally," and that often underscored the United States commitment to Israel's security, buttressed the relationship.

The pattern of strategic cooperation established in the Reagan administration did not expand during the Bush presidency. It was tested during the international crisis and war spawned by Iraq's invasion of Kuwait in August 1990. The United States asked Israel to keep a low profile that would avoid giving Saddam Hussein a tool with which to split the anti-Iraq coalition. When President Bush asked that Israel not respond to the Iraqi Scud attacks, Israel complied. At the same time, the administration turned to other regional states, especially Turkey and Egypt, for both military forces and logistical support. Although the logic behind this approach was evident, it raised questions both in the Congress and in public perceptions about Israel's strategic value and utility in supporting U.S. interests and policies in the region.

With the end of the Cold War and in the aftermath of the Gulf War, the United States refocused on achieving a just, lasting, and comprehensive peace between Israel and its neighbors, including the Palestinians, and on achieving viable security arrangements to assure regional stability and unimpeded commercial access to the vast oil reserves of the Arabian Peninsula and Persian Gulf. These have been among the basic goals of the United States in the region during much of the post–World War II era and take an added significance in the 1990s and into the twenty-first century.

The Middle East contains most of the world's known oil reserves and will continue to be a growing source of oil for the United States, Japan, and Europe well into the future. High levels of oil consumption, limited proven reserves, and the absence of an effective national energy policy have contributed to a heavy and growing United States dependence on imported, especially Middle Eastern, oil. Petrodollars have also made the oil producing states a valuable commercial and financial prize. Beyond the rationale for ending the Arab-Israeli conflict as a goal in itself, there is the argument that ending the conflict would reduce regional instability that might inhibit access to oil.

Whatever Israel's strategic value to the United States may have been before the end of the Cold War, the situation has clearly changed with its end and the collapse of the Soviet Union and the end of the Communist threat. However, U.S.-Israel strategic cooperation never was premised solely on countering the Soviet threat; both states took a broader approach, despite the relatively narrow wording of their formal agreements.

One school of thought is that Israel never was a true strategic asset in the East-West conflict because it could not be called on to send a division to fight in the Ukraine or in Europe, and if it had been called on, its impact would have been marginal. Nevertheless it could play a regional role by providing intelligence analyses of Arab world developments as well as information concerning captured Soviet and Soviet bloc equipment following the 1967, 1969–70, 1973, and 1982 wars. Although the latter value has clearly diminished, Israel can still provide useful intelligence and it has been helpful in ensuring the survival of some, especially moderate pro-Western Arab regimes, as with Jordan in 1970.

The rise of political Islam in North Africa, the resurgence of the independent Muslim republics in Central Asia, and the regional activities of the Islamic regimes in Sudan and Iran suggest that Islam in its political or militant variant (commonly referred to as Islamic fundamentalism or Islamism) may take the place of international communism as a threat to U.S. interests in the Middle East and beyond. But does it, in fact, constitute a serious challenge to the United States, and if so, will it be a factor in the evolving strategic relationship between the United States and Israel presenting an opportunity for further cooperation? Some Muslim political leaders and groups, such as the Hezbollah in Lebanon and the Hamas movement in the occupied territories, have used religion to mask the espousal of violence, extremism, and terrorism. But Islam is a legitimate expression of religious beliefs, not a movement supported by a coordinated international effort to change societies according to the rules of a militant version of Islam. If those who advocate societal reform to conform to the teachings of Islam pursue this goal largely within the framework of a democratic process and broader political participation and are not antagonistic to their neighbors or to the West, the United States will not be hostile. If, however, democratic processes are subverted and Islamists come to power only to destroy that process and become confrontational, such as in the cases of Iran or Algeria, this will likely evoke United States opposition.

Thus, at least in the immediate period, Islamic fundamentalism is not an alternative to the Soviet communist menace as a focal point of U.S.-Israel strategic cooperation. A new conflict between Islam and the Westt has not replaced the East-West rivalry of the Cold War. Although there is not yet a substitute for the anti-Soviet strategic value identified in previous concepts and incorporated in such documents as the MOUs, Israel remains a potential asset to the United States in other respects. The precise nature and dimensions of such a role have not yet been fully defined, but it may, for example, be of continued value in combatting terrorism.

ISRAEL'S SURVIVAL AND SECURITY

In a press conference on May 12, 1977, Jimmy Carter said: "We have a special relationship with Israel. It's absolutely crucial that no one in our country or around the world ever doubt that our No. 1 commitment in the Middle East is to protect the right of Israel to exist, to exist permanently, and to exist in peace. It's a special relationship."[6]

Since Israel's independence, the United States has had an interest in its survival and security, although this has not always been a priority focus of U.S. policy. The underlying arguments have concentrated on shared values and historical association, but there has also been strategic utility and intangible values. Henry Kissinger argued:

I think there's a moral commitment to Israel which does not derive from the fact that it is a strategic asset even though it is *also* a strategic asset. Because when all is said and done, it is the one country which we can be sure will never change its friendship for the United States, and which in a foreseeable crisis represents a relationship of fundamental strategic importance.[7]

Although there is a widely perceived commitment to Israel's survival and security, the nature of that commitment and the means to implement it remain imprecise.

Israel has no mutual security treaty with the United States, nor is it a member of any alliance system requiring the United States to take up arms on its behalf. It is assumed that the United States would come to Israel's assistance were it to be gravely threatened, but there is no assurance that it will do so. During the Gulf War, in 1991, when Israel was under Scud missile attack from Iraq, the United States sent a small number of troops to Israel to operate the Patriot missiles. Nonetheless, the extent of the U.S. commitment to Israel, beyond providing diplomatic and political support and military and economic assistance, remains ambiguous. The commitment has been couched in the generalized form of presidential statements rather than formal accords. Although such statements reaffirmed U.S. interest in supporting the political independence and territorial integrity of Middle Eastern states, including Israel, they do not commit the United States to specific actions in particular circumstances. In 1969 the Senate Foreign Relations Committee noted:

Consider, for example, the widely held view that the United States is committed to the defense of Israel even though we have no security treaty with that country. The source of this alleged commitment is in fact nothing more than a long series of executive policy declarations, including: President Truman's declaration of support for the independence of Israel in 1948; the British-French-American tripartite declaration of 1950 pledging opposition to the violation of frontiers or armistice lines in the Middle East; President Eisenhower's statement of January 1957 pledging American support for the integrity and independence of Middle Eastern Nations; Secretary of State Dulles's assertion of February 1957 that the United States regarded the Gulf of Aqaba as an international waterway; President Kennedy's press conference of March 1963 pledging American opposition to any act of aggression in the Middle East; and President Johnson's statements of February 1964 indicating American support for the territorial integrity and political independence of all Middle Eastern countries.

All of these declarations are executive policy statements; not one is based on a treaty ratified by the Senate. The only treaty commitment the United States has in the Middle East is as a signatory to the United Nations Charter.[8]

In more recent years, the U.S.-Israel arrangement has been codified to some extent in specific documents associated with the Sinai II accords (1975), the Egypt-Israel Peace Treaty process, the 1981 Memorandum of Understanding on Strategic Cooperation, and subsequent similar arrangements. Sinai II and the Egypt-Israel Peace Treaty, particularly the accompanying U.S.-Israel letters and memoranda, placed the United States role on a more precise footing. For example, the memorandum of agreement between Israel and the United States, dated September 1,

1975, which accompanied the Sinai II accords and was signed by Secretary of State Henry Kissinger and Israeli Deputy Prime Minister and Minister of Foreign Affairs Yigal Allon, stated:

In view of the long-standing United States commitment to the survival and security of Israel, the United States Government will view with particular gravity threats to Israel's security or sovereignty by a world power. In support of this objective, the United States Government will in the event of such threat consult promptly with the Government of Israel with respect to what support, diplomatic or otherwise, or assistance it can lend to Israel in accordance with its constitutional practices.

This pledge was similar to that made in other U.S. alliances and treaties that focused on the Soviet threat. The United States also spelled out its position regarding the PLO,[9] pledged to use its veto in the United Nations Security Council to prevent alterations in the accords, and gave assurances on economic and military assistance. However, the Sinai II guarantees did not establish a formal and legally binding United States commitment to military action on Israel's behalf.

The United States commitment centered on the survival of Israel against implacable enemies. This led Israel's decision makers to believe that the United States would not permit a major Soviet military action against it and would act to deter the USSR from becoming significantly involved in regional conflict, but Israeli leaders were not similarly certain about the nature and extent of United States support of its position in an Arab-Israeli context. Although they believed that the United States would ensure Israel's security and integrity, they did not interpret the commitment too broadly.

Accompanying the Egypt-Israel Peace Treaty of 1979 were memoranda of agreement that reaffirmed and broadened the United States' assurances provided to Israel in connection with the Sinai II accords, including economic and military assistance and assurance of Israel's oil requirements.

Has the U.S. commitment to Israel changed since the end of the Cold War? Despite the changes that have occurred in the nature of the threat to Israel's security, the commitment appears as strong as it was before the emergence of the post–Cold War new world order. In June 1992, Assistant Secretary Djerejian noted: "we remain unshakably committed to Israel's security and to preserving Israel's qualitative edge over any likely combination of aggressors."[10] This formulation rehearsed a long-standing U.S. policy on two major elements of the strategic connection.

ARMS TRANSFERS AND THE ARMS BALANCE

Arms transfers to Israel and the maintenance of the arms balance between Israel and its regional adversaries have been salient elements of the strategic connection since before the establishment of the state of Israel. The United States' role as arms provisioner evolved from that of nonparticipant (the United States adopted an arms embargo in 1947) to that of principal supplier of modern, sophisticated military equipment, beginning in the late 1960s. The United States has become indispensable in this regard, as alternative suppliers of essential military equipment for Israel are not readily available.

In 1947 the United States embargoed the shipment of arms to Palestine as well as to neighboring areas. The embargo was not lifted after the Arab-Israeli War of 1948–49, and in May 1950 the United States joined with Great Britain and France in the Tripartite Declaration that sought to control the flow of arms and to prevent the development of an arms race in the Arab-Israeli zone. The United States was eager to avoid being identified as a partisan in the Arab-Israeli conflict and becoming extensively involved in the region. Consequently, the Tripartite Declaration remained the basis of United States policy until the mid-1950s when it was made irrelevant in light of France's arms supplies to Israel and the Czechoslovakian-Egyptian arms deal of 1955. When the latter was announced an alarmed Israel, faced with implacable Arab hostility, worried that the danger of conflict would increase were its military position to deteriorate. Israel sought arms to maintain the military balance between itself and the Arabs, especially Egypt, and made requests for specific arms from the United States. The administration refused to entertain these requests and Israel turned to alternate suppliers, including France, Canada, and England. The United States indicated that it would not object to these countries supplying Israel with arms, the underlying rationale being that although it wished to avoid becoming a principal arms supplier, it also did not want to see a regional arms imbalance develop, either. It tempered its reluctance with occasional supplies to Israel of limited quantities of "purely defensive weapons," such as the sale of HAWK missiles in 1962, following the disclosure of a large shipment of Soviet arms to Egypt, Syria, and Iraq.

During the Johnson administration, the United States became more involved in the supply of military equipment, such as Patton tanks, to Israel as well as to the moderate Arab states but emphasized that it was refraining from becoming a major arms supplier while helping the regional states to meet their defense requirements through occasional, selective sales.

Thus, by the eve of the Six Day War, the United States had emerged as a limited supplier of weapons to Israel. Nevertheless, at the outbreak of hostilities, it imposed an arms embargo on Israel and the Arab states that lasted until October 1967, when it announced that it would release selected items of military materiel to Israel, Lebanon, Saudi Arabia, Morocco, Libya, and Tunisia. Immediately after the war, the United States sought to prevent a Middle Eastern arms race from developing by achieving an understanding with the Soviet Union on regional arms supply. This objective was included in President Lyndon Johnson's Five Principles of Peace and was a subject of discussion at the Glassboro Summit between Johnson and Alexei Kosygin in June 1967. The failure to achieve such an understanding or to incorporate this idea in United Nations Security Council Resolution 242,[11] coupled with Israel's inability to secure jet aircraft from France, intensified the pressure on the United States to become involved in the supply of arms to Israel in order to maintain the regional military balance. Subsequently, the United States role as an armorer of Israel became increasingly important and arms supply and the military balance became a major subject of the U.S.-Israel dialogue.

Israel sought to buy supersonic F-4 Phantom jets. To maintain the balance, the United States agreed to provide Israel with additional HAWK missiles and to deliver the Skyhawk A-4 subsonic fighter bombers Israel had bought before the war. Washington's initial response to Israel's request for Phantom jets was negative. After considerable discussion and political maneuvering, the State Department announced on December 27, 1968, an agreement to sell Israel 50 Phantom F-4 jets. This was a major turning point: thereafter, Israel became almost totally dependent on the United States for sophisticated military equipment. At the time, the United States and Israel also agreed on the need to maintain a military balance (operationally defined as Israeli qualitative military superiority) in the Arab-Israeli sector. This led to periodic discord concerning the existence of arms imbalances and the means to address them. Israel was soon seeking additional quantities of F-4 Phantom jets, A-4 Skyhawks, and HAWK missiles from the United States, as well as economic assistance to help offset the strains on its economy caused by post–Six Day War defense expenditures.

As the War of Attrition along the Suez Canal intensified and Soviet aid to Egypt continued, and with reports of Soviet pilots flying operational missions for Egypt, there was increased pressure on Washington to supply Israel. The escalating danger impelled the United States, in June 1970, to take an initiative to stop the shooting along the Canal and to start negotiations. At the same time, President Nixon underscored the importance of maintaining Israel's military superiority in order to prevent further conflict, and the United States provided Israel with additional military equipment and accelerated some shipments under existing contracts.

In the wake of Israeli complaints about Soviet-Egyptian violations of the August standstill cease-fire, the United States announced, in early September, that it would monitor the military balance closely to ensure that Israel's security would not be adversely affected and would begin a continuing effort to "rectify" breaches of the agreement. "Rectification" was to restore Israel's confidence through additional military supply, and included a pledge by Nixon to keep the arms pipeline open.

In the fall of 1971, Secretary of State Rogers proposed an interim Suez Canal agreement. Prime Minister Golda Meir pointed out that although the United States had helped to maintain the military balance, the supply of planes to Israel had been interrupted, while significant amounts of Soviet arms and equipment were being supplied to Egypt and Syria. Israel, therefore, linked its participation in the interim agreement negotiations with the supply of Phantom jets. In January 1972, after long discussions, the United States reassured Israel that it would not seek to impose its views on the substance of a settlement and agreed to sell it F-4 Phantom and A-4 Skyhawk aircraft over a period of several years. At the same time, it became known that earlier the United States agreed to provide Israel with technical assistance in the manufacture of defense equipment to help it become more self-sufficient in producing major weapons systems.

By the time the Yom Kippur War erupted, the United States had become Israel's principal and virtually sole source of sophisticated weapons systems. The United States commitment to Israel's security was reflected in the type, sophistication, and value of the military equipment it provided to Israel. The commitment was graphically demonstrated by U.S. military supply during and immediately after the war. During hostilities, the U.S. supplied Israel in order to redress the military imbalance resulting from the massive Soviet airlift of military equipment to Syria and Egypt and to replace the substantial losses suffered by Israel in combat. The U.S. airlift was of military, political, strategic, and psychological importance to Israel. On October 19, 1973, Nixon asked Congress to provide $2.2 billion in emergency security assistance for Israel, including direct military grants.

After the war, the United States maintained its role as the principal supplier of military equipment to Israel based on the concept of maintaining the military balance to prevent war, to assure the security of Israel, and to promote a settlement of the Arab-Israeli conflict. The United States also became more extensively involved in the sale of increasingly sophisticated equipment to traditional Arab clients as well as to new Arab customers such as Egypt. The 1978 "package deal," which included the sale of F-5E aircraft to Egypt, F-5E aircraft to Saudi Arabia, and an increase in the number of F-15s that had already been pledged to Israel, was a major watershed in terms of providing access to the U.S. arsenal for both Egypt and Saudi Arabia at sophisticated levels and in amounts that they had not previously contemplated. This deal was soon overshadowed by the decision in 1981 to allow Saudi Arabia to buy AWACS aircraft worth $8.5 billion and to enhance the capability of its previously acquired F-15s. This deal was a major turning point in the U.S. role as an arms provider to the Arab states.

Israel's concerns about growing Arab access to the U.S. arsenal already apparent in the package deal and AWACS debates were enhanced by U.S. decisions to provide substantial arms to Jordan. Prime Minister Begin focused on this as a "grave threat" to Israel's security and argued that should Jordan receive the proposed equipment Israel "will be in direct, real and severe danger." Reagan sought to reassure Begin in a letter made public on February 16, 1982: "I am determined to see that Israel's qualitative technological edge is maintained and am mindful as well of your concerns with respect to quantitative factors and their impact upon Israel's security."[12]

The discord that characterized much of the discussion about arms transfers in the decades before the Reagan administration took office faded with the signing of several memorandums of understanding in the 1980s. Nevertheless, the lack of perfect policy congruence on a number of issues affected the flow of arms (suspensions of deliveries, disagreements over the kinds of equipment to be supplied and over delivery timetables, and the effect of equipment deliveries by the United States and others to the Arab states on the military balance).

During Ronald Reagan's tenure, the United States increased sales of sophisticated equipment to both Israel and those Arab states committed to the West and to policies of moderation and who were opposed to the Soviet Union and its regional machinations. At the same time the United States sustained and enshrined in its rhetoric the principle, articulated in Reagan's 1982 letter to Begin, that it would continue to assure Israel's qualitative edge.

Despite broad agreement between Israel and the United States regarding Israel's defensive arms requirements and the necessity of sustaining Israel's qualitative edge, discord concerning specifics has arisen on numerous occasions. Israel and the United States have often disagreed about the level of the threat Israel faces. Israel generally bases its assessment on a worst case scenario and on the assumption that it may have to face the combined strength of its Arab adversaries. Although the United States acknowledges that there is a threat to Israel from its Arab neighbors, it often believes that Israel overstates the threat. Recently, this has meant that Israel has not adjusted its threat assessment to take into account the post–Cold War and post–Gulf War realities, which include the significant influence wielded by the United States in many of the Arab states and Syria's loss of the Soviet Union as its patron and armorer, despite some recent supplies of high-technology equipment from the former Soviet Union and bloc states.

They have also disagreed over the definition of qualitative edge: Israel has generally seen this in terms of the transfer of high-technology weapon systems to itself before they are offered to the Arab states, giving it a clear technological lead over possible adversaries until the next generation of technology advances is available. Since the early 1980s, however, the time lag between the delivery of high technology weapons systems to Israel and to the Arab states has shrunk considerably. The United States sees Israel's definition as too limited and feels it should be broadened to include not only weapons technology but military training, leadership, intelligence, alliances, morale, infrastructure, doctrine, strategy, and motivation. The U.S. perspective is that, even without the transfer of additional high technology weapons, Israel's qualitative edge will continue to improve through the end of the 1990s.

U.S. strategic cooperation with the Arabs has been a growing source of friction. The United States, focused on the issues of regional stability and internal strife, believes in the need to create an effective self-defense capability in friendly Arab states, to encourage the formation of effective collective security arrangements, and to plan for external reinforcement of friendly Arab regimes in times of crisis. This requires the sale of high technology weapons as a force multiplier to compensate for these states' low personnel resources and to permit them to face enemies with advanced weapons systems. Israel questions these sales as inconsistent with the commitment to maintaining its qualitative edge.

An example of the dilemma arose when, soon after a highly visible and positive meeting between Prime Minister Rabin and President Bush in August 1992, the U.S. administration announced it would sell 72

F-15E aircraft to Saudi Arabia. Rabin noted his opposition, saying that his government would object strongly if the United States sold warplanes to Saudi Arabia because that would upset the military balance in the Middle East and would require Israel to add to its own arsenal to keep pace. Bush acknowledged that he had considered the implications for stability in the Middle East, including the need for Israel to maintain its qualitative edge over Arab military capabilities. Rabin saw it as futile to try to prevent the sale and chose instead to concentrate on compensatory arms acquisition.

United States' sensitivity to Israeli concerns led it to couple Bush's announced decision with a letter, signed on October 1, by Secretary of Defense Richard Cheney that pledged the transfer of Apache attack and Blackhawk utility helicopters to Israel. Those were transferred under the Congressionally mandated $700 million drawdown to Israel. In November 1993, President Clinton offered Israel 24 F-16 A-B fighter aircraft worth $160 million to complete the $700 million drawdown, and pledged to support additional Congressional drawdown legislation to transfer an additional 24 F-16s.

Nonetheless, Israel's qualitative edge has become increasingly difficult for the United States to maintain through the transfer of military hardware alone. It is virtually impossible to find the resources to balance large United States arms transfers to the Arab world with greater sales to Israel. Under current fiscal conditions it would be extremely difficult for any administration to seek an enlargement of United States aid to Israel with which it would pay for additional compensatory armaments, and Israel cannot afford to engage in an arms race with the wealthy Gulf Arab states. Previously established patterns of arms supply to Israel and the maintenance of its qualitative edge are likely to be sustained for the foreseeable future. However, Washington's decision to take a more prominent role in the security of the Persian Gulf and to enhance the military capabilities of the Gulf Cooperation Council member states will further complicate the stated United States goal of ensuring Israel's qualitative edge.

WEAPONS PROLIFERATION

Nuclear nonproliferation has been a declared policy objective of the U.S. government since World War II. During his presidential campaign, Bill Clinton spoke of the need of keeping weapons of mass destruction (nuclear, biological, and chemical) out of the hands of Iran, Iraq, Syria, and Libya. At the same time, he reiterated a strong commitment to maintaining Israel's qualitative military edge. Furthermore, Israel was noticeably absent from the list of potential abusers of such weapons. In general, the United States has tried to prevent the nuclearization of the Middle East through diplomatic efforts. Except for very brief periods, however, and despite the rhetorical emphasis on the subject from one administration to another, nonproliferation has not been high on the U.S. policy agenda for the Middle East or elsewhere, and Washington's approach has been equivocal and inconsistent.

It is widely believed that Israel has nuclear weapons, although this has never been officially confirmed or proved. Israel has not announced a nuclear weapons program, nor does it advocate the desirability of nuclear weapons, nor is there overt evidence of a deployed Israeli nuclear force. However, given its ambiguous nuclear policy statements, its refusal either to deny or confirm reports about its nuclear activities, and its refusal to adhere to the Non-Proliferation Treaty or otherwise accept safeguards on its nuclear program, Israel conveys a strong impression that it possesses a nuclear-weapons capability. It is widely assumed that Israel either has a high option for the production of nuclear weapons or has already produced a limited number of such weapons.

Since undertaking its nuclear program in the 1950s, Israel has not acknowledged the existence of a weapons program. This policy has allowed Israel to give the impression that it has the capability to produce nuclear weapons while limiting the dialogue with the United States on the issue and reducing the pressures on Arab and Islamic states to acquire such weapons themselves. Israel's standard policy statement is a model of ambiguity: "Israel will not be the first to introduce nuclear weapons in the area."

Israel has not permitted international inspection of its nuclear facility at Dimona, and it will not contemplate opening up its program, much less dismantling it, without first achieving peace with its neighbors and viable regional arms control agreements. It insists that stringent verification procedure must be set up in such states as Algeria, Libya, and Iran, which it believes are actively trying to acquire nuclear weapons. It also is concerned about Pakistan's so-called "Islamic bomb." Israel is officially committed to a Middle East nuclear free zone and, if peace is achieved, it can renounce nuclear weapons as unnecessary. In an interview in *Davar* on April 17, 1992, Rabin said:

Israeli governments have on more than one occasion declared our willingness to make the Middle East a zone free of nuclear arms and other weapons of mass destruction, based on a mutual agreement between Israel and each of the countries of the region. This position remains in effect, although Iran would have to be included today in any such agreement.

In January 1993, during the signing of a convention to ban chemical weapons, Foreign Minister Shimon Peres, for the first time by an Israeli leader, explicitly called for a mutually verifiable zone free of surface to surface missiles and chemical, biological, and nuclear weapons but only after peace is achieved and a nuclear ambitious but hostile Iran is included.

Although all post–World War II U.S. administrations have been seized with the issue of nuclear proliferation, there has been relatively little effort to confront Israel on this subject. Eisenhower reportedly told Israel that he wanted Dimona to be subject to international inspection, but he accepted Israeli government assurances that the reactor would not be used to pursue a nuclear weapons program. After the *New York Times* reported in December 1961 that Israel was building a nuclear reactor that could produce weapons-grade plutonium, President Kennedy accepted Prime Minister David Ben Gurion's assurances that Israel intended that the nuclear reactor would be used only for peaceful research purposes. President Jimmy Carter came into office with nonproliferation on his agenda, and the Nuclear Non-Proliferation Act of 1978 was passed in his administration, but his focus in the Middle East was on the peace process and the Egypt-Israel Peace Treaty. On June 7, 1981, Israel bombed the Osirak nuclear reactor in Iraq and the United States joined in a unanimous Security Council resolution condemning the attack. However, when the International Atomic Energy Agency attempted to isolate Israel within the agency, the United States walked out in protest and Congress froze funds for the agency until its board of governors certified that Israel would be allowed to participate as a member. The Reagan administration did not respond to a number of public revelations about Israel's nuclear advances.

In May 1991, President Bush outlined a Middle East arms control initiative that called on all states in the region to support a ban on the production of nuclear weapons materials, but the administration's position on Israel's nuclear program was equivocal. On May 8, 1992, Central Intelligence Agency Director Robert Gates noted that, unlike the efforts by Iran and some of the Arab states, Israel's nuclear program was protective in nature — that Israel had developed its "deterrent and defensive capabilities as hedges against the Iranian and Iraqi threats." This benign assessment was consistent with the general United States view. Later that year, Gates contrasted Israel with three unfriendly regimes (Iran, Iraq, and Libya) whose acquisition of nuclear and other nonconventional weapons and related delivery systems would threaten United States interests: "Arsenals all too often [are] in the hands of megalomaniacs, military governments, strongmen of proven inhumanity, weak and unstable governments, or in the hands of some who are threatened by such governments."[13] The Middle East was an area of special concern, but Gates did not include Israel in his list of those contributing to the proliferation of weapons of mass destruction.

Over the years neither the executive branch nor Congress has taken significant measures concerning Israel's nuclear program. Despite rumors, revelations in the media, the assessments of various government agencies, and leaked reports about Israel's program, there has been no public acknowledgment that it even exists, no U.S. administration has launched a high-profile campaign against Israel, and no punitive action has been taken. Challenging Israel's nuclear program might threaten Israel's strategic doctrine and its regional defense strategy. The key has been Israel's policy of ambiguity. So long as Israel does not publicly acknowledge that it has a nuclear capability, the United States does not have to openly address the question of how that capability might impinge on U.S. interests or face any difficult policy choices. Israel's keeping the "bomb in the basement" has facilitated the U.S. position. There is no need to respond to rumors. If Israel were to detonate a nuclear warhead or were to proclaim publicly that it had nuclear weapons, however, the United States would be compelled to respond.

Although the 1992 Democratic party platform contained a pledge to curb proliferation, Bill Clinton sent a mixed message on arms control and proliferation. Clinton noted that Israel was surrounded by nations pursuing weapons of mass destruction, was at risk of Scud attacks by Iraq, and faced a Syria armed with more advanced Scuds. These and related observations made after Clinton took office, as well as Israel's coy approach to its nuclear activities, suggest that at least in the short term the focus on Israel's nuclear posture is unlikely to emerge as a major issue in the special relationship.

THE NEW STRATEGIC CONNECTION

In April 1990, Congressman Les Aspin addressed the question of whether, given the changes in East-West relations, U.S.-Israel relations were likely to diminish. After noting that in the 1980s the United States had signed three formal agreements with Israel and President Reagan had issued a national security decision directive establishing a joint political-military group, and after listing a wide range of cooperative strategic and military efforts, Aspin concluded, "Quite simply, the demise of the Cold War should not change our strategic relationship with Israel."[14] He argued that the relationship was not premised on the Soviet threat but on Israel's strategic needs to cope with the Arab threat, and it is based on the strategic needs of the United States that have not involved any Soviet threat in the Middle East in recent years.

In many respects we are now in a period very much like the one that followed World War II, when the construction of a new world order required the reassessment of existing policies and the generation of new working assumptions. It is, therefore, instructive to recall that in the initial debates on the effects of the establishment of a Jewish State in Palestine, the overwhelming view in the Departments of State and Defense was that Israel would be a strategic liability hindering U.S. access to oil and spoiling relations with the peoples of the Arab and Muslim worlds. The argument was based on the assumption that the conflict between Israel and the Arab-Muslim world would be a zero-sum game. Later, especially during the Reagan administration, Israel was identified as a strategic asset of singular significance to the United States. Both positions — and the assumptions underlying them — were overstated. Although Israel has not been an unalloyed asset, neither has there been a palpable negative effect on the United States role in the Arab world because of its connection to Israel. From the 1940s to the 1980s, policy profferers argued that support of Israel is an element in a zero-sum game that would adversely affect United States interests in and relations with the Arab and Muslim worlds. Some analysts have sustained this argument into the 1990s, and while there are examples to support this proposition, the preponderance of evidence suggests that it is not the dominant outcome. Despite long-standing suggestions that there is an either/or choice between Israel and the Arab states (or, often, Arab oil) developments have shown that there is no requirement for such a choice.

The connection with Israel has not precluded relationships with the Arab states, nor has it necessarily compromised the quality of those links. On the contrary, U.S.-Israel ties have illustrated the overall value and reliability of U.S. commitments, including those in the Arab world.

The special relationship has also reinforced the position of the United States as the only viable external factor in the quest for an Arab-Israeli peace. Washington's participation was crucial in achieving the cease-fire agreements in 1970 and again in 1973; the disengagement agreements between Israel and Egypt and Israel and Syria in 1974; the Sinai II accords in 1975; the Camp David Accords in 1978; the Egypt-Israel Peace Treaty in 1979; the cease-fire that ended the Lebanon War in 1982; the May 17, 1983, agreement between Israel and Lebanon; the convening of the Madrid Peace Conference of 1991; and the sustaining of the subsequent bilateral and multilateral negotiations. And, of course, in the wake of the Oslo secret talks, it was the United States to which Israel and the PLO turned to assure implementation of the Declaration of Principles. The U.S. relationship with Israel was instrumental in generating the level of influence in the region needed to broker these processes that was never attained by the anti-Israel and pro-Arab Soviet Union (despite the visibility as co-chairman often granted it by the United States, the Soviets and, now, the Russians, were and are informed about, but not significantly involved in, the process) nor by the more neutral European Community.

Despite Arab hostility to Israel, the United States has increasingly strengthened its links with the Arab states. Arab states accept U.S. aid, purchase U.S. military equipment, receive U.S. technical assistance, and, despite the Arab boycott of Israel, do substantial business with, and sell oil to, the United States and other friends and allies of Israel. Israel has even been seen as an ally of sorts for the more moderate Arab states in their confrontations with radical elements in the Arab world and beyond. For example, in the 1960s, Israel helped to thwart Egypt's ability to pursue President Nasser's expansionist efforts in the Arabian Peninsula and the Persian Gulf. This was recognized by some of the threatened Arab states and by the Shah of Iran, who regarded Israel as a reliable, if essentially covert, ally in the effort to prevent radical Arab expansion. Because it was in their interest to do so, Arab states turned to the United States for assistance — Jordan in 1970, Egypt for its encircled Third Army in 1973, and Kuwait and Saudi Arabia after the 1990 Iraqi invasion. The Gulf War clearly illustrated the point that the United States connection with Israel is not a liability. Arab states joined the coalition, and remained in it, despite Bush administration concerns that one or more of them might withdraw because of the Israel connection.

The Arab world does not today present the United States with an either/or choice with regard to two dominant regional interests: oil and Israel. The special relationship has had no significant adverse effect on U.S. access to Middle Eastern oil, with the exception of the 1973 oil embargo. There is no reason to believe that even if Israel were to disappear this would result in a significant reduction in the price of oil or a meaningful increase in access to the region's petroleum resources. There are many factors that affect oil price and supply, notably the political and economic interplay of Organization of Petroleum Exporting Countries and their individual needs for income, that outweigh the Israel factor. Images of a repeat embargo similar to 1973 inevitably haunt those concerned with oil availability, but for a variety of reasons, including diversification of sources, such an embargo would be more difficult to institute and sustain than it was in 1973. There are significant Arab investments in the West and the industrialized world is now better prepared to respond to an embargo. Indeed, since the summer of 1990, some Arab states have invested considerable sums to increase oil production and ensure adequate flows to the United States and its allies, while continuing to restrain prices. This occurred as the United States reasserted its commitment to Israel's survival and security, continued to provide it with military and economic assistance, and maintained its role in the peace process.

Nevertheless, there will be an ongoing debate and conspiracy theories will be advanced arguing that the special relationship is neither natural nor to the advantage of the United States (nor to Israel), but rather it is a consequence of the United States pandering to "special interests" that seek to sustain a relationship for other and less noble reasons. The conspiracy theories seek to explain the darker side of the relationship. Often containing some elements of truth, they tend to rely on unsubstantiated evidence, and while the arguments seem logical they often lack supporting testimony. The difficulty is proving that something did not occur or to substantiate and document the counterargument.

Many of the Arab and Muslim states appear to be reconciled to the U.S. connection with Israel despite continuous, and sometimes vigorous and visible, protests of Israel's policies and of U.S. support of them. For some there is the recognition of the reality of the new world order. With the Soviet Union out of the picture, it is clear that the United States represents the only realistic source of economic and military assistance and political-diplomatic support. The Gulf War drove this point home. King Hussein of Jordan appeared to recognize this factor in reorienting his policies after the end of the war, as did Hafez al-Assad in committing Syria to participate in the U.S.-sponsored peace process and in his desire for an enhanced dialogue with the Clinton administration.

But if Israel cannot be said to be a strategic liability for the United States, does the converse hold? Can it be said to be an asset? Israel continues to be of value in the counterterrorism arena and a useful source of intelligence concerning the Arab world, as well as in other spheres. Intelligence cooperation can be traced to the early 1950s and liaison continues to be a mutually beneficial relationship. Special episodes of particular benefit followed the Six Day War when Israeli successes enabled it to provide copies of, and information about, captured Soviet military equipment. Other advanced equipment was provided over the years. They continue to share information, although each does not share all that is available. Israel is also a potential partner in defense-industrial development. The United States military and the defense industry have benefitted from Israel's experience with U.S. weapons and specific suggestions for enhancements and improvements. Israeli weapons technology has also been made available to the United States. This will continue, although this value may be diminished by increasing U.S. concerns over transfers of U.S. technology to third countries. Israel continues to be a site suitable for ports of call by U.S. vessels, as a potential training site for U.S. forces, and as a location for the maintenance and repair of U.S. vessels. Israel's technological contributions to the development of weapons systems are complemented by the value and utility of its intelligence.

Nevertheless, it is unlikely that the future ties will be posited on the concept of Israel as a strategic asset because of the difficulty of identifying specific potential situations in which Israel might be more than a marginal actor. Apart from providing intelligence, participating in scientific/technological exchanges, making its facilities available, and allowing the prepositioning of equipment on its soil, Israel's role will be limited. Contingencies in which the Israel Defense Forces might play a prominent role are hard to imagine. The Gulf War confirmed the self-fulfilling perspective of President Bush, Secretary of State James Baker, and National Security Adviser Brent Scowcroft, who did not see Israel as a strategic asset. In areas such as intelligence gathering, prepositioning of U.S. equipment and materiel, and logistical facilities, the United States preferred to rely on alternative sources rather than have even indirect involvement of Israel in the conflict. The fear of alienating its Arab partners emerged as Bush's major concern, outweighing a perspective of Israel as strategic asset. This led some to conclude that the crisis confirmed the strategic irrelevance of Israel to the United States in dealing with inter-Arab crises. In the discussions on the shaping and structuring of the new world order, the strategic role of Israel remained, at best, peripheral.

The Gulf War did not establish a new paradigm for strategic cooperation between the United States and Israel as did previous conflicts in the region. It suggested a continuity in the U.S. approach, at least in the Bush tenure, that would mark the links in the 1990s. The sending of U.S. soldiers to Israel to operate the Patriot missiles was a very special case, and unlikely to set a precedent for future action. Israeli restraint in response to U.S. entreaties was an aberration that probably would not be repeated in future similar circumstances, given the trauma and results of the decision to do so in 1991. At the operational levels of the Pentagon, the perspective derived from the Gulf War experience reinforced earlier views that Israel was too far removed from the zone of combat and too loaded with political baggage to be an important or even useful player in a war focused on the Gulf sector. Whether this Pentagon-held and Bush administration supported dual perception of an Israel of little value and with the potential to disrupt the coalition by its very participation was a valid one will never be known, because it was not tested. While the arguments might continue in both directions, a strong case can be made for the alternate view that Israel would have been a useful, if not valuable, participant, and that its involvement would not have disrupted the coalition — Arab regimes under threat would not have been particularly concerned about the source of the military capability to ensure their survival, as long as they survived the onslaught. In any event the conclusion drawn by the Arabs and others was that Israel proved to be strategically irrelevant and that there were Arab states that could and would prove to be strategic allies of the United States in the region (Egypt being the prominent example).

The disintegration of the Soviet Union, the collapse of the Warsaw Pact, and the limited value of Israel's role in the Gulf War have raised further questions about the marginalization of Israel in the security realm. Both the United States and Israel project a reduced conventional military threat to Israel over the next few years, as well as a reduced level of threat in those areas of the Middle East where Israel might be a valuable strategic asset.

Possible Israeli arguments for its continued strategic value could include a role as a base for prepositioning U.S. materiel for use in regional contingencies or Israeli cooperation against the possible emerging threat of Islamic fundamentalism. Whether this prepositioned equipment would be utilitarian in potential contingencies depends on the nature of the situation. Given a growing U.S. military focus on the Gulf and continued negotiations with the states of that sector to preposition equipment to supplement that afloat on naval vessels and on Diego Garcia, there is a U.S. military perspective that does not perceive equipment in Israel as well positioned for probable contingencies in the Gulf sector. There is a continued concern that Arab states would be reluctant to accept U.S. assistance that came from or through Israel.

Israel remains a valuable intelligence asset gathering important information in the region. It is a major ally in the effort against terrorism. It gains information and has developed counterterrorist techniques of use to the U.S. effort. Military equipment that has been prepositioned for potential use by the United States serves a utility.

In reassessing the strategic relationship, it is important to separate rhetoric, even at the presidential level, from the reality at the working levels among those charged with implementing these concepts of greater strategic cooperation between the United States and Israel. Liberalization of technology transfer rules is unlikely. Haifa is unlikely to become a home port for the Sixth Fleet even while there will be a continuation of port visits and joint exercises and training. Large scale prepositioning of equipment for U.S. military use is unlikely.

Whether Israel is or is not a strategic asset of the United States, the strategic connection remains critical, especially to Israel. It is clear and beyond debate that the United States is and should remain committed to the survival and security of the State of Israel. To assure Israel's security without a direct U.S. commitment of forces, the military supply relationship remains the decisive alternative. Israel has sought and, after a slow evolution to that point, it has been U.S. policy to provide the arms and related materiel essential for the Israel Defense Forces to ensure the survival and security of Israel. Increasingly this has been subsumed under the rubric of "maintaining Israel's qualitative edge" over its Arab adversaries. Even as it pursues efforts to achieve an Arab-Israeli peace, the United States will need to sustain the strategic links that ensure Israel's survival and security through military supply and maintaining the qualitative edge, whether or not Israel is a strategic asset to the United States, in order to achieve peace and reduce the threats to the broader U.S. interests in the Middle East.

4

The Political Component of the Special Relationship

Politics is an instrumental factor in the special relationship, not its basis. The U.S. political process is the means through which the underlying factors — the ideological-emotional components and strategic connections — of the special relationship are converted into policy and actions. From its outset, the special relationship has had a political component.

In democratic systems, domestic politics — political participation, voting behavior, and public opinion — influence foreign policy. In the United States, a strong domestic constituency composed of various groups including, but not limited to, the American Jewish community has created and sustained a policy interest in Israel and has advocated its case. Although the pro-Israel forces are sometimes mislabeled "the Jewish lobby," it is useful to recall that some small Jewish groups (such as Neturei Karta and American Jewish Alternatives to Zionism) and some individual Jews do not support Israel, while various Christian groups (such as the National Christian Leadership Conference for Israel and the International Christian Embassy) are advocates for the Jewish state. At the same time a strong and vocal group centered on, but not limited to, the Arab-American community, contests U.S. policies and opposes Israel's special position. Wooing the Jewish vote and courting Jewish political activists and financial support are elements of U.S. politics. Presidential candidates often make efforts to secure the Jewish vote as a means of winning electoral support in crucial states where there are large blocks of Jewish voters, just as they woo the support of other voting blocks within the U.S. electorate. Candidates for political office often proffer promises concerning the United States-Israel relationship, although the realities of Washington and the responsibilities of office tend to cause delays, modifications, and avoidance of implementation of pledges. How much of Israel's success with Congress and the executive branch can be attributed to the Jewish vote, Jewish financial support of pro-Israel candidates, and the influence of Jewish politicians?

THE AMERICAN JEWISH COMMUNITY

The American Jewish community continues to be Israel's main moral, economic, and political support group in the United States. Most individual American Jews demonstrate a concern for Israel, as do virtually all the major American Jewish organizations. American Jews are not the first or the only religious or ethnic group to seek to influence U.S. policy toward their coreligionists or kinsmen abroad. Focused ethnic-religious advocacy applies to Irish, Polish, Greek, Catholic, Italian, and other groups with varying degrees of intensity and success. Nevertheless, perhaps more than any other U.S. group, American Jews express an attachment to a foreign state (Israel) and few are as absorbed or concerned by events thousands of miles away in the Middle East.

The American Jewish community, the world's largest and most influential, numbers about six million, or 2.4 percent of the population of the United States. Jews live in every state, with the largest proportion concentrated in the northeast, generally in urban centers. The community is heterogeneous, informed, and politically active, especially on issues related to Israel and with respect to issues of social justice, equality, and anti-Semitism. Its members are generally better educated, of a higher social status, and more engaged in philanthropic activity than the average American.

The community is well organized. Traditionally, community relations agencies and federations were the focal point of many Jewish communities, but identification has shifted in recent decades from the agencies concerned exclusively with traditional causes, such as anti-Semitism and separation of church and state, to those concerned with Israel. Israel has become the central issue for the American Jewish community. Large memberships, well-trained professional staffs, substantial financing, and effective programming and communications characterize the major American Jewish organizations, which form a network linked through a number of national umbrella organizations, such as the Council of Jewish Federations and the National Jewish Community Relations

Advisory Council. This network is able to mobilize responses to issues of concern to the Jewish community in a cohesive and rapid way. No one individual or group speaks for the entire American Jewish community, with perhaps the exceptions of the American Israel Public Affairs Committee (AIPAC) and the Conference of Presidents of Major American Jewish Organizations.

The American Jewish community is engaged in an ongoing effort to influence U.S. policy toward Israel, to build cultural and social bridges between itself and Israel, and to foster links between the two societies as a whole through numerous avenues ranging from tourism to philanthropy. Members of the American Jewish community show support for Israel in a number of ways, including direct financial support amounting to hundreds of millions of dollars annually through Jewish philanthropic agencies, as well as by hundreds of thousands visiting Israel each year. There is a steady flow of Americans to Israel who participate in all aspects of Israeli life and who facilitate the cultural exchanges between the two states. Large numbers of prominent U.S. political figures and other celebrities travel to Israel, as do ordinary tourists. Israelis travelling to the United States provide a people to people connection that enhances the policy climate. There is a connection of Jewish leaders and Israeli diplomats revolving around a special concern and commitment and their shared Jewishness.

The American-Israeli Jewish connection has been a factor in creating a U.S. presence in Israel. Virtually every important Israeli educational, medical, cultural, scientific, research, and philanthropic institution is supported in some, often significant, way by American Jewish aid (and, in some cases, by U.S. government aid as well). Israelis representing governmental, political, economic, cultural, scientific, and educational institutions, as well as students, trainees, and tourists have also travelled to, and many have lived in, the United States. U.S. culture has had such an impact on Israel that in some respects it is possible to say Israel has been "Americanized."

Zionism is a focus of Judaism. The Bible, Jewish writings, and Judaism concentrate on Zion and Jerusalem. Zionism as a spiritual movement has deep roots in Jewish history and tradition; Zionism as a political movement is of relatively recent origin. The leadership of political Zionism was primarily European until World War II, when the Holocaust lent additional credence and urgency to the Zionist efforts, and American Jews became more active in the movement. The American Jewish community debated the very necessity of a Jewish state before

Israel's independence, and diverse perspectives — Zionist, anti-Zionist, and non-Zionist — developed and were sustained even after 1948.

The Six Day War and the crisis that preceded it dramatically altered the importance of Israel in American Jewish thinking. The threat to Israel's existence galvanized American Jews, and ambivalence within the American Jewish community virtually ended. Virtually the entire Jewish community was concerned about and supported Israel — a reaction more widespread and deeply felt than had been anticipated. After the war and Israel's overwhelming victory, the interdependence of Israeli Jews and Jews of the Diaspora, especially American Jews, became more obvious. The Yom Kippur War reinforced the "Zionization" of the American Jewish community. Israel's fate has become inextricably intertwined with American Jewish life and identification with Israel became a central characteristic of American Jewry.

Support for Israel dominates American Jewish public life, is part of the American Jewish consensus on what it means to be a Jew, and is voiced by a large majority of American Jews. News about Israel dominates Anglo-Jewish newspapers and periodicals and is the mainstay of community annual fund-raising campaigns of Jewish philanthropic organizations. On the other hand, only a small proportion of American Jews express a passionate involvement with Israel, and fewer still think about immigrating to, and settling in, the country. In general, many American Jews do not have a detailed and differentiated knowledge of developments in Israel nor is its culture a significant part of their lives.

Despite their small numbers relative to the overall U.S. population, American Jews have had a disproportionate influence on the electoral process. A number of factors account for this, including the concentration of Jews in states with a high number of electoral college votes; a high rate of participation in elections; experience, skill, and sophistication in organizing political activities and articulating group interests; effective fund raising and generous financial mobilization for political causes; and an Israel-related concentration of political efforts. Jews contribute more generously to political campaigns than do other ethnic groups; a higher percentage of Jewish voters goes to the polls than any other group.

In 1992, nine states (California, Connecticut, Florida, Illinois, Maryland, Massachusetts, New Jersey, New York, and Pennsylvania) with large Jewish populations held 202 presidential electoral votes of the 270 required for victory. Because Jews tend to be more politically active than the overall population, they gain a multiplier effect for their votes and exert an influence out of proportion to their actual numbers. Important supporters of Israel are among the prominent supporters of presidential candidates.

In the past, individual Jews were among the most important financial backers of political candidates and active fundraisers of the major political parties. Campaign reform laws have modified their relative importance in recent years, but Jewish donations to political causes continue to be out of proportion to population percentages and to their relative wealth. Like other groups, American Jews have also created numerous political action committees (PACs) through which they have funneled substantial funds to favored candidates, especially members of committees that approve aid to the Middle East. The political effect of Jewish PAC money is difficult to gauge, but the concentration on a single foreign policy issue, rather than a number of diffuse subjects, gives the funding more weight.

The historical significance of American Jewish support for Israel is clear. The question is: How reliable and solid is the American Jewish community as a base of support or as an advocate for Israel?

The Jewish community continues to show a passionate and wide-spread concern for, and remains strongly supportive of, Israel, although it does not always agree with particular policies of its government. American Jews distinguish between concern for Israel and support for Israeli government policy. Although the greatest disenchantment appears to be found among Jews who are far removed from organized Jewish life, the leadership of the American Jewish community seems to be rethinking the exact nature of its support. More committed Jews find less to fault in Israeli policies, and hard-core critics of Israel form only a small, albeit vocal, minority of American Jews.

American Jews are experiencing a rise in intermarriage, a decline in Jewish teaching and practices, and a weaker attachment to Judaism. These factors may well cause a weakening of the Jewish community as well as of its attachment to Israel. Assimilation leads to decreases in community membership and funding and reduces the organizations' abilities to influence policy. When this happens, organizational resources must be reallocated to deal with these issues rather than being used for Israel-oriented activities.

The new generation of the American Jewish community seems to be less inclined to unquestioning support for Israel. The relationship between the organized American Jewish community and Israel changed between 1977 and 1992, during the tenures of Prime Ministers Menachem Begin and Yitzhak Shamir. Despite the American Jewish community's deeply held and broadly shared perception of security threats to Israel and a shared commitment to Israel's existence, security, and well-being and to mobilization on behalf of continued U.S. economic, political, and military assistance to Israel, there was a lack of unanimity on the territorial outcome of peace and on measures taken by Israel in response to the intifada and other security questions. Support for Israel remained strong although there was growing criticism within the Jewish community on specific matters, an anguish about Israel and its policies in the occupied territories, and because of its perspective on the peace process. There were doubts about Israel's policies concerning the War in Lebanon, the Pollard affair, and the election of Rabbi Meir Kahane to the Knesset in 1984. There was also discord concerning Soviet Jews over whether to support the emigration of the Soviet Jews totally or their emigration only to Israel, how to handle their resettlement in Israel, and the associated matter of settlement construction in the occupied territories and loan guarantees. The perennial "Who is a Jew?" debate became particularly problematic during the process of government formation after the 1988 Knesset election.

Notwithstanding such alienating issues and events, continuity and stability in pro-Israel sentiment among American Jews was clear, even while impressionistic evidence indicated an increase in public criticism. In the immediate aftermath of the Gulf War and the Scud missile attacks on Israel, American Jewish worries about Israel's security and wariness of Arab intentions increased. Quantitative surveys show that American Jews have grown more attached to Israel and the return of Rabin to power intensified this affection, as the Labor Party's policies, especially in relation to the ongoing peace process, seemed to be more in line with American Jewish preferences.

American Jewish support for Israel appears firm, although in the longer term its durability should not be taken for granted. Accord between the two communities may prove particularly difficult as Israel focuses on the specific issues in the peace process such as the future of the West Bank, the Gaza Strip, the Golan Heights, Jerusalem, the settlements, and their inhabitants. American and Israeli Jewry perceive continuing threats from a largely hostile neighborhood, and the American Jewish community accepts the basic logic of Israel's security concerns. Moreover, American Jews are convinced that only a strong Israel can serve as an incentive for its adversaries to pursue peace. They are supportive of Israel's national consensus on the question of the indivisibility of, and continued Israeli sovereignty over, Jerusalem. But some vocal elements in the United States have questioned the wisdom of Israel's refusal to make unilateral concessions (for example, a temporary freeze on settlements) or to wholly accept the territories-for-peace formula. Some elements in the American Jewish community reject the Likud-espoused concept that continued unrestricted control over these territories is indispensable to Israeli security.

The Jewish vote in the 1992 U.S. presidential election is illustrative of the orientation and role of the American Jewish community. As usual, the Jewish population turned out to vote in larger proportions than the general population. They returned to the Democratic Party and showed strong support for Clinton as the community apparently believed that Israel would be better served with Clinton as president and supported his domestic agenda. Bush lost about one-half of his previous Jewish supporters; his support among Jews dropped from the 30 percent that he garnered in 1988 to between 10 and 15 percent in 1992. In part, this was attributed to his posture on Israel, including his lack of appreciation for Israel's restraint during the Gulf War, and his linkage of the $10 billion in loan guarantees to halting the settlements in the West Bank and Gaza Strip. When, in his September 1991 news conference, he seemed to deny that U.S. citizens had the right to lobby for the loan guarantees, he angered even those who agreed with him on the settlements issue. The dominant and overriding issues for many Jewish voters were domestic concerns: the economy, jobs, health care, the deficit, abortion, and education. Foreign policy ranked at the highest levels for only about 6 percent of the Jewish electorate — a level lower than the population at large.

Jewish Democratic voters made significant contributions to Clinton's victory in several key states and nationwide. The general conclusion is that Jewish voters continued to play a crucial role in politics, especially Democratic politics and at the grassroots level, far disproportionate to their numbers. The high Jewish voter turnout was an important factor. Although by 1992 Jews accounted for only about 2.4 percent of the population of the United States, they accounted for 4 percent of the overall vote and between 6.4 percent and 7 percent of Clinton's total national vote. In key states, Jewish votes (an estimated 78 to 85 percent of the Jewish vote went to Clinton) were a significant component of the Clinton vote and may well have affected the outcome of a number of important races in crucial states.

THE PRO-ISRAEL LOBBY

An influential pro-Israel lobby, primarily but not solely Jewish in composition, functions within the parameters of the U.S. political system, exerting influence on policymakers and the policy process to sustain the U.S.-Israel special relationship. It is composed of diverse organizations whose activities and concerns relating to Israel range from cultural, educational, and religious to philanthropic, financial, and political.

The Israel-oriented American Jewish organizations fall into two broad categories: those engaging primarily in fund raising, and those focusing on educational, public relations, or political activity. American Jewry has materially aided the establishment, development, and consolidation of Israel through outright philanthropic gifts and the purchase of Israel bonds. Over the decades this has involved tens of billions of dollars. The American Jewish community has also been involved in extensive cultural, social, educational, public relations, and political activities on behalf of Israel in the United States. Although the community is well organized and highly structured, it is very complex, and neither monolithic nor hierarchical. No one organization or individual can claim to represent American Jewry, but when the issue is Israel-oriented, AIPAC and the Conference of Presidents are in the forefront, although others often pursue their own, generally but not wholly parallel, courses.

The Conference of Presidents is an umbrella organization and coordinating body of the major American Jewish organizations with diverse concerns that include fraternal matters, community relations, civil rights, religious themes, philanthropic activity, social welfare, and Zionist issues. Originally created in the mid-1950s to present a consensus perspective and to prevent the overlapping of response on matters affecting Israel, it had a relatively minor role until the Six Day War. With the "Zionization" of the American Jewish community in 1967 came the increased need for coordination of the various interested groups, and the Conference became more significant as a mechanism for contact and consultation between Israel and American Jewry. Nevertheless, there are numerous other issues on the Jewish agenda.

The Conference seeks to develop a consensus on issues of major concern to the Jewish community. The members discuss, consult, and coordinate their activities, but they must be unanimous to act, and they speak as a group only when they have achieved a consensus. They present this perspective to the White House, the State Department, foreign embassies, and their memberships for their information and, often, for their action in meetings and with materials. The Conference and its component organizations also seek to interpret Israel to the U.S. body politic, and to explain the United States to Israeli officials. Many of its component organizations are often active and vocal themselves on

Israel-related issues, thereby reinforcing the work of the Conference. Besides its meetings with high-level officials, the Conference is also an important element in the public relations arena where it seeks to mobilize Jewish and non-Jewish support for Israel at both local and national levels. Events must be interpreted so that they are understood by the general, as well as Jewish, populations; political action and public education are important factors in creating favorable climates and policies.

At the core of the pro-Israel lobby is AIPAC, which concentrates on Congress. AIPAC represents, is responsible to, and articulates the consensus of the organized American Jewish community.

U.S. supporters of Israel early on recognized the need for an official, permanent American Jewish pro-Israel lobby in Washington. The American Zionist Committee for Public Affairs was established in 1954 and renamed the American Israel Public Affairs Committee in 1959. It assumed the task of "co-ordinating and directing public actions on behalf of the American Zionist movement, bearing upon relations with governmental authorities, with a view to maintaining the improving friendship and good will between the United States and Israel." Originally it was a small organization discreetly lobbying Congress, but this began to change in the 1970s as Jewish communities and their leaders sought a mechanism to work politically for improved U.S.-Israel relations. Jewish leaders joined AIPAC as individuals and its power and visibility grew. In the 1980s it began to become a mass membership organization with regional and sub-regional units, and it increased its political activities at national, state, and local levels. It now has more than 55,000 members.

AIPAC is unique among American Jewish organizations. Despite its acronym, it is neither a political action committee nor a foreign agent, and it does not lobby for the state of Israel. It is a legally registered, U.S. domestic lobbying organization working to facilitate, maintain, and improve relations between the United States and Israel. It is not tax exempt and it is supported by private contributions from U.S. citizens. It seeks to represent the concerns of Israel's supporters in the United States in the context of what is in the best interests of the United States. AIPAC activists operate in areas where there are large concentrations of Jews as well as in regions where few Jews are found. AIPAC deals directly with Congress and the executive branch to facilitate aid and other assistance to Israel. Its publications are widely distributed as a source of information and analysis of United States policy concerning Israel and the Middle East, and it acts as a conduit of information and attitudes among

American Jewry, official Washington, and the broader U.S. domestic political environment on matters of concern to its constituency.

AIPAC's ability to provide reliable and accurate information to Congress in a prompt manner has enhanced its reputation. Its staff has helped to draft speeches, write legislation, advise on tactics, perform research, collect cosponsors, and marshall votes. AIPAC also monitors the Washington bureaucracy and Congressional hearings, tracks legislation, and keeps records of members' votes, statements, and actions concerning Israel and the Middle East. At times administrations have sought AIPAC's help in lobbying for portions of the foreign aid bill not related to the Middle East.

AIPAC's success derives from a number of factors. Its members often seek to elect and reelect politicians friendly to its position and to develop relationships with rising political figures. It seeks to establish and sustain a network of sympathetic, cooperative Congressional aides. Congressional aides are not only the repositories of institutional memory and the technical expertise, they are the ones who do much of the work, and often are the ones who draft the legislation, prepare the amendments, organize the hearings, write the reports, and help plan the strategy. AIPAC's goal is to ensure that these aides are provided with reliable information, workable strategies, and the support they require. It has also worked to develop and nurture a grassroots system of individuals who have access to members of Congress, are committed to strong U.S.-Israel relations, and are willing to take an active role in promoting them.

AIPAC employs a multitude of direct and indirect methods. It establishes personal contacts with influential politicians, Congressional aides, administrative assistants, advisers, and bureaucratic officials. Its personnel testify before Congressional committees and subcommittees. AIPAC organizes letter writing and other public relations campaigns to supplement these actions. The ability of pro-Israel groups to form coalitions with other domestic elements and to secure endorsements from such diverse sources as prominent public figures; African-American, Asian, and Hispanic leaders; scholars; entertainers; and celebrities has helped to enhance the special relationship.

Estimating the strength and precise impact of AIPAC is difficult. What might have been had the lobby not been part of the political process is impossible to determine. Its record in facilitating the adoption of pro-Israel measures in Congress is difficult to quantify with precision but generally its perceived power is enviable. Although some of the legislation would probably have been adopted in any event, it can be argued that AIPAC probably has initiated the ideas and assisted in sustaining the sentiment and support.

AIPAC is an effective and efficient operation that has been remarkably successful in attaining its primary objective — the enhancement of the bilateral relationship between the United States and Israel. U.S. military and economic aid is a tangible accomplishment. It enjoys a number of advantages in its efforts among which the most significant is a sympathetic operational environment. U.S. leaders have said the relationship is in the U.S. interest and the emotionally-shared values legacy of U.S. history has contributed to the positive framework. Americans in general have been sympathetic toward Israel.

AIPAC's successes have generated copy-cat organizations favoring other policy objectives, criticism from various sources about its methods and activities, and various legal challenges. Its leadership has not always been cohesive and a series of inappropriate comments and actions caused much turmoil among its professional and lay leadership in recent years. Among the most sensitive areas has been the area of rewarding friends and punishing "enemies" in Congress.

There is a widely held view that the pro-Israel lobby is powerful enough to ensure the defeat of members of Congress who choose not to support pro-Israel positions or who have been problematic and unhelpful on issues of importance to the lobby. Direct claims by AIPAC or others to have defeated members of Congress are extremely rare, although there are former members who argue that AIPAC and its supporters "defeated" them, among them former Representatives Paul Findley and Paul McCloskey and former Senator Charles Percy. While all are vocal about their defeat at the hands of the lobby and the lobby has noted a role in their ouster, the claims are probably exaggerated.[1] AIPAC does not engage in political activity favoring a particular party nor is it directly involved in election campaigns. However, AIPAC does disseminate information regarding the voting records, levels of support for Israel, and public statements of candidates that may well influence the votes and campaign contributions of its membership.

AIPAC's past successes lend it an aura of power. Over time, it has achieved a series of important successes, concentrated in two broad areas: sustaining economic and military assistance levels to Israel, even in times of economic distress and deficit reduction pressures in the United States, and in limiting arms transfers to the Arab states. It can be argued, as high administration officials have noted, that overall foreign aid packages have often been approved by Congress because of the strong sympathy for Israel and the need to ensure that aid for Israel would be available. AIPAC's success in building bipartisan support for Israel is such that a number of measures are routinely approved by Congress without the need for extensive or intensive activity by AIPAC.

THE POLITICAL COMPONENT IN THE FUTURE

The political factor will continue to be significant and the lobby, despite recent tensions, will continue to use the political instrument to enhance U.S.-Israel relations.

On September 12, 1991, George Bush challenged the pro-Israel lobby openly by stating that $10 billion in loan guarantees to Israel would contribute to the further extension of Israeli settlements in the occupied territories, a policy he strongly opposed as an obstacle to peace. The unprecedented attack by Bush on the lobby's role in promoting the special relationship was an important and prominent event that is unlikely to be of lasting significant consequence. He feared that Congressional consideration and probable approval of the guarantees would negatively influence Arab decisions to participate in the peace process. He sought to delay Congressional action by claiming to be "one lonely little guy" seeking to overcome "powerful political forces," a thinly veiled allusion to the pro-Israel lobby. Although he stressed his undiminished support for Jewish immigration to Israel as well as for the security of the Jewish state, he noted that "too much is at stake for domestic politics to take precedence over peace. This I know is something the bulk of the American people understand."[2] In an address to AIPAC's annual policy conference on April 5, 1992, Tom Dine, then its Executive Director, accused Bush of "[questioning] the inalienable right of American citizens . . . to lobby on this issue. September 12, 1991, will be a day that lives in infamy for the American pro-Israel community."[3] The president prevailed on this issue, despite considerable opposition in both the Senate and the House, primarily because he evoked the national interest, presidential prestige, and the potential success of United States policy. But this was an aberration and required the expenditure of a considerable amount of political capital on an issue where Israel and its supporters were far from monolithic in its position.

In assessing the future of political support one must take into account that strains in the connection between the American Jewish community and its Israeli counterpart have always existed and have periodically surfaced, despite continuing fundamental support. The argument is generally tactical, not strategic, in nature and this pattern will continue and may intensify at times. There are significant differences between the

Israeli and American Jewish communities in outlook and perspective. Financial support from the United States is significant and substantial. Israelis often feel that American Jews respond only with checkbooks and not with their presence — either temporarily as tourists at crucial times or as new immigrants. The difference in perspectives derives from a number of factors, including the fact that for most Israelis the Diaspora is not regularly on their minds. In times of crisis the Israeli expects the Diaspora to come to his assistance, but beyond that there is not much thought on the matter. The opposite is true of American Jews, for whom Israel is a major factor in their Jewish identity and Israel's survival is of great concern. Although the United States still has the world's largest Jewish community, Israel's position as the second largest continues to grow. Given the combined factors of Soviet Jewish immigration to Israel and intermarriage and assimilation in the United States, the Jewish center of gravity is shifting to Israel. It is likely that in the first decades of the twenty-first century the largest Jewish community will be in Israel rather than in the United States.

Prime Minister Rabin and his closest advisers appear to believe that American Jewish organizations should not play a central role in the bilateral diplomatic relationship. He prefers government-to-government diplomacy that places him wholly in charge. During an August 1992 visit to the United States, Rabin, in a private meeting with AIPAC officials, reportedly berated them for needlessly straining U.S.-Israel relations by engaging in losing battles. In a public speech to Jewish leaders he was curt in his insistence that decisions affecting U.S.-Israel relations are made in Jerusalem. Clearly, he envisions a different role for American Jews in maintaining the special relationship, preferring a Rabin-centered, hands-on approach. This contrasts with the American Jewish community's self-perception as a significant actor influencing and facilitating the relationship.

Rabin's criticism of AIPAC should be placed in context; his political style is fundamentally different from those of his predecessors. He is more involved and direct in his approach and prefers one-on-one diplomacy with the U.S. president (as demonstrated by his several meetings), a style that draws on his personal and professional background as Chief of Staff of the Israel Defense Forces, ambassador to the United States, and Prime Minister. Rabin negotiated and reached agreement directly with Secretary of State James Baker by telephone in the fall of 1992 on compensation for the proposed U.S. arms sale to Saudi Arabia, and with Secretary of State Warren Christopher in the winter of 1993 on the Hamas deportees. Rabin apparently believes this is an efficient and fruitful mechanism even if it diminishes the importance and power of the lobby. Rabin sees the executive branch as the focus of attention and of more importance than the Congress in matters of foreign policy.

Nevertheless, Congress today plays a greater role than it did in the early 1970s when Rabin was ambassador to Washington, and the American Jewish community has learned how to use its political power effectively. The realities of dealing with new administrations in both Jerusalem and Washington have affected the nature of the lobbying dynamic but not its objectives. Bush's attack on AIPAC and his success in shaping the debate on the loan guarantees, combined with Rabin's criticism of AIPAC, raised questions about AIPAC's ability to represent Israel's perspective and preferences in political outcomes among its members and its lobbying targets on Capitol Hill and elsewhere. The restoration of a close, but not identical, perspective held by the Labor-led government and AIPAC was already clear by the March 1994 AIPAC policy conference. Rabin told AIPAC that he brought "the heartfelt gratitude of the State of Israel and its citizens" and summarized his attitude with the observation: "I am a friend of AIPAC. We may have differences, but I would like to say we have many friends and many support organizations throughout the world. AIPAC has been, and will remain, the spearhead of the special relations between Washington and Jerusalem."[4] Senators and representatives believe AIPAC is important and potent and that AIPAC will retain an influential role in Congress. The lobby and the broader American Jewish community will continue to be crucial in generating and sustaining political support for Israel even while its operational dynamic will be altered by the new personalities and the political processes they establish as well as by the issues they address. The American Jewish community and the lobby will continue to make United States policy more favorable to Israel than it would be without such activity.

CONGRESS AND ISRAEL

The President and the executive branch generally dominate the foreign policy process, but Congress has been especially active and effective concerning Israel and the Middle East. Over the years, Congress has become increasingly assertive and better informed on matters concerning Israel's security and well-being, which remains salient on Capitol Hill in which partisan division plays little or no role.

Congressional interest in Israel antedated the independence of the Jewish state and can be traced to World War I and the British Mandate in

Palestine, and even earlier. In September 1922 Congress unanimously approved the Lodge-Fish resolution endorsing the Balfour Declaration: "the United States of America favors the establishment in Palestine of a national home for the Jewish people." Numerous political figures and other prominent Americans articulated support of the concept in succeeding decades.

Once Israel became independent, it began to turn to Congress for understanding and support in its efforts to influence the policies of the executive branch. The relationship between Congress and Israel slowly took on a multifaceted and complex nature, with many examples of Israel receiving special and preferential treatment. It receives high levels of economic and military assistance and is the only state that receives its economic assistance in cash at the outset of the fiscal year. It is also permitted to use part of its military assistance in Israel rather than in the United States. Israel may also compete for United States defense contracts.

Israel has become a filter or prism through which Congress assesses other states relations with the United States. Arms sales to the Arab world are more closely scrutinized because of concern for Israel's security. Actions concerning the Soviet Union and the Soviet bloc were often affected by their relations with Israel. Thus, for example, the Jackson-Vanik amendment (1974) conditioned improved United States-Soviet Union economic relations in part on Moscow's internal treatment of Jews and on allowing them to emigrate. In the 1980s, Ethiopia and the Sudan were subjected to close scrutiny of their actions concerning the Ethiopian Jews (Falashas) and their ability to emigrate to Israel. Congress looked more carefully at relations with and aid for states based on their support of the United Nations resolution equating Zionism with racism. Some legislation was modified to ensure that Israel would not be detrimentally treated. Pro-Israel actions of members often seek to force changes in administration policy that they deem damaging to Israel, and they encourage the executive branch to support Israel in international forums, such as the United Nations and other organizations, where its position has been in jeopardy.

Congressional support for Israel has been consistently strong, especially after the Six Day War, as indicated in numerous resolutions, votes, statements, cosponsors on resolutions, public statements, letters for public release, and other instruments. Generally, resolutions and statements favorable to Israel have had substantial numbers of co-sponsors. Support is broad-based, not confined to representatives coming from Jewish population centers, and includes Republicans and Democrats as well as conservatives and liberals.

Foreign aid (economic and military assistance) has become a measure of Congressional support. Israel has been the beneficiary of Congressional efforts to increase, and, later, to sustain, its levels of economic and military assistance. The conditions under which such aid is provided are perhaps even more important than the $1.8 billion in forgiven Foreign Military Sales credits and $1.2 billion in Economic Support Fund assistance provided annually in recent years. This includes the earmarking of these levels of aid to reduce administration discretion and the numerous amendments that exist concerning specific programs for Israel, such as early disbursing of the funds. In these and related activities the pro-Israel lobby has played an important part in sustaining the levels of aid and the preferential policies regarding disbursement. Congress often has been more favorable to Israel than the executive branch and has increased assistance levels beyond those requested by the president. It has granted lenient loan repayment terms and the conversion of loans to grants. Congress at times has initiated new foreign aid programs to Israel's benefit, such as providing funds for the resettlement of Soviet Jews in Israel. It has included prohibitions in the aid bills to prevent assistance to other states that might prove harmful to Israel. Congress also has used legislative measures and other, more indirect, means to influence administration policy on Israel's behalf, including letters, statements, and sense of Congress resolutions, as well as Committee hearings and reports designed to influence policy. Among the most prominent of these is the letter of May 1975 in which 76 senators wrote to President Ford concerning U.S. policy (discussed in more detail below).

Support for Israel has also led Congress to give careful scrutiny to appropriations and military sales to Arab states, which often are approved with limiting conditions following significant and sometimes embarrassing (to the Arab states) debate — such as the Airborne Warning and Control System (AWACS) decision in 1981. Congress has also passed legislation governing compliance with the Arab boycott of Israel in an attempt to undercut its effectiveness.

Congressional involvement in policies with respect to the Middle East has not been limited to the exercise of the power of the purse. Congress has taken broader initiatives to restrict the administration's Middle East policy and to support Israel's preferred political posture. In June 1967 the Senate approved the Symington-Javits resolution calling for a stable and durable peace in the Middle East. A Ribicoff-Scott statement of April 25,

1969, called for face-to-face negotiations between Israel and the Arab states. A Case-Tydings declaration of February 25, 1970, called for direct negotiations between Israel and the Arabs and restated the principle that Israel's deterrent strength must not be impaired. A letter of May 26, 1970, to Secretary of State William Rogers urged the United States to provide additional jet aircraft to Israel. In July 1970, 72 senators sent a letter to President Nixon citing the increasing Soviet role in and on behalf of Egypt and supporting a policy to deter the Soviet role. In September 1970, the Senate defeated, by a vote of 87 to 7, an amendment to the Military Procurement Act that would have prohibited authorization for the transfer of military equipment to Israel by sale, credit sale, or guarantee. On July 31, 1971, the Senate passed, by a vote of 76 to 9, a Jackson amendment to the Military Procurement Act authorizing the president to transfer to Israel by sale, credit sale, or guarantee such aircraft and other equipment as necessary to counteract military aid to other Middle Eastern states. On November 23, 1971, the Senate voted 82 to 14 to approve an amendment to the Defense Appropriations Act appropriating $500 million to enable the president to provide sales or credit sales of weapons to Israel, including $250 million specifically for F-4 Phantom aircraft. On May 12, 1982, the House approved by a vote of 401 to 3 a sense of the Congress resolution stating that if the United Nations General Assembly "illegally" expelled or suspended Israel from either the General Assembly or specialized United Nations agencies, the United States should withhold its contribution or suspend its own participation in the General Assembly or agency in question. On December 9, 1974, 71 members of the Senate wrote to President Ford and urged "that you reiterate our nation's long-standing commitment to Israel's security by a policy of continued military supplies, and diplomatic and economic support."

In May 1975, 76 senators wrote to President Ford reaffirming their support for Israel:

We believe that the special relationship between our country and Israel does not prejudice improved relations with other nations in the region. It is imperative that we not permit the military balance to shift against Israel. . . . We trust that your [foreign aid] recommendations will be responsive to Israel's urgent military and economic needs.

On November 11, 1975, both houses of Congress unanimously called for a reassessment of the United States relationship with the United Nations and condemning the vote of the General Assembly equating Zionism with racism. When the Carter administration issued a joint communique with the Soviet Union on October 1, 1977, concerning Middle East peace, 136 members of the House sent a letter to the President expressing "grave concern" about reintroducing a Soviet role in the Arab-Israeli peace efforts and urging him to reaffirm support for United Nations Security Council Resolutions 242 and 338 and to affirm the basic commitment to the "well-being of Israel within secure and defensible borders." When the Carter administration later hesitated to endorse the Sadat initiative and the Sadat-Begin efforts to further the peace process, Congress passed a concurrent resolution commending the two leaders and supporting their efforts. In June 1989, 95 U.S. senators wrote to Secretary of State James Baker "to express our support for the peace initiative recently launched by the Government of Israel."

Efforts in Congress to restrict the flow of arms or aid to Israel or in other ways to limit the relationship generally have fared poorly. In 1973, for example, Senator J. William Fulbright's attempt to withhold a portion of Israel's aid package until Israel took steps to comply with certain United Nations resolutions was defeated 62 to 12. In 1976 Congressman David Obey sought to cut military credits for Israel and was defeated 342 to 32. In 1979, Senator Mark Hatfield sought to cut military credits to Israel and was defeated 78 to 7. Although the Senate supported President Reagan on the proposed AWACS sale to Saudi Arabia in 1981, the House voted 301 to 111 against the president. In 1991 an attempt by Congressman Valentine to eliminate a Gulf War grant to Israel was defeated, 397 to 24.

In 1977, Congress cut the foreign aid appropriations by 11 percent but approved the full amount of economic and military assistance requested for Israel and added unrequested funds to aid in the resettlement of Jewish refugees in Israel. It also changed the mix of economic assistance to increase significantly the amount of cash budgetary assistance. In considering the FY 1983 economic and military aid requests, Congress approved a foreign aid package for Israel that included $510 million more in grant aid than the administration had sought.

Congressional support for Israel has been especially conspicuous in the area of arms sales, where it has helped to assure that Israel remains a preferred recipient of U.S. arms. Congress has closely monitored the regional arms balance and has been mindful of Israel's needs. Although Congress has not vetoed any administration's arms sales proposals, the power has been important in restraining the executive branch. Indeed, on several occasions the potential of a Congressional veto has brought controversial sales to the focus of public debate. In 1975, for example, President Ford yielded to Congressional pressure and replaced Improved (mobile) HAWK anti-aircraft missiles with regular HAWK batteries in a proposed sale to Jordan. In 1976, Congressional opposition forced the Ford administration to reduce sharply the number (from 1,500 to 650) of television-guided Maverick air-to-ground missiles to be sold to Saudi Arabia for use on F-5E combat aircraft. In 1978 the Carter administration, in order to secure passage of its proposed arms package for Israel, Egypt, and Saudi Arabia, pledged that Saudi Arabia would not be provided with AWACS, that its F-15s would be based outside striking distance of Israel, and that they would not be equipped with conformal fuel tanks, Sidewinder air-to-air missiles, or bomb racks. When, in 1981, President Reagan reversed Carter's pledge and proposed selling Saudi Arabia five AWACS and other equipment including conformal fuel tanks and Sidewinder missiles, he set off a heated debate. Following an overwhelming vote of disapproval in the House, and a letter of disapproval cosponsored by a majority of senators, Congress came closer than ever to vetoing an administration-proposed arms sale, but the weight of presidential prestige narrowly prevented that outcome. In 1985 the Reagan administration proposed a multibillion dollar arms sale for Jordan. Nearly three-quarters of the Senate introduced a resolution voicing disapproval of the sale and later voted 97 to 1, and the House unanimously, to delay the sale for a hundred days or until "direct and meaningful peace negotiations between Israel and Jordan are underway." The administration subsequently postponed the arms sale indefinitely.

The generous scope of aid to Israel, even in this era of high budget deficits, reflects the widely held belief that a strong, economically viable, and stable Israel is in the interest of the United States. This helps to explain why Congress approved, in May 1986, the U.S.-Israel Free Trade Area Agreement and implementing legislation by a vote of 422 to 0 in the House and by a unanimous vote in the Senate.

The extent of Congressional support for Israel once led Senator William Fulbright to complain, on "Face the Nation," on October 7, 1973, that "the Israelis control the policy in the Congress and the Senate." The Fulbright view is exaggerated, although analysis of legislative activity indicates a strong and widespread pro-Israel consensus in the Senate and the House. Pro-Israel strength and support in Congress has been such that, at times, various administrations have used it as a policy locomotive to help secure Congressional action in other areas. Aid for junta-controlled Greece (1967-74) was secured with the argument that support of Israel required facilities in Greece. Aid to Cambodia in 1973 was coupled with legislation providing emergency aid to Israel to facilitate Congressional approval. When Senate Foreign Relations

Committee Chairman Richard Lugar took the foreign aid authorization bill to the Senate floor in 1985, he began his presentation by announcing that it called for $1.5 billion in emergency economic aid for Israel. The amendment passed unanimously. Lugar's tactic acknowledged that aid to Israel is a Congressional priority and could help to secure the entire foreign aid package.

Throughout the years, Congress has been unable to impose its own coherent policy on the executive branch but has been influential, if not always successful, in restraining, modifying, and supplementing administration policies in a pro-Israel direction, although this support has not been uncritical. In March 1988, a bipartisan group of 30 senators, including some of Israel's strongest and most prominent supporters, sent a letter to Secretary of State George Shultz strongly endorsing his peace efforts and expressing their dismay at Prime Minister Shamir's refusal to accept the "land for peace" formula as a basis for peace. Such public chastisement of Israel was rare, and it troubled Shamir, but was welcomed in the White House. In recent years, there have been suggestions of unease and differences between the views of members of Congress and some of Israel's policies and a greater willingness by members of Congress, and Congressional staff, to criticize Israel in public. Most notably these have revolved around the question of settlements and Israel's response to the intifada. This has coincided with a growth in concern for Palestinian and broader Arab grievances. Congressional concerns have been expressed in private discussions, Congressional hearings, and even in occasional public statements. Nevertheless, the strength of Congressional support for Israel — if resolutions, votes, and appropriations of aid are any indication — shows no significant erosion. If there is a chasm between public declaration on the one hand, and "behind closed door" sentiment on the other, it remains to be manifest in public action.

EXPLAINING CONGRESSIONAL SUPPORT: IDEOLOGY AND POLITICS

This is not to suggest that Congress supports Israel for no better reason than fear of the Israel lobby; on the contrary, I know of few members of either house of Congress who do not believe deeply and strongly that support of Israel is both a moral duty and a national interest of the United States. It is rather to suggest that, as a result of the activities of the lobby, congressional conviction has been measurably reinforced by the knowledge that political sanctions will be applied to any who fail to deliver.[5]

The foundation of Congressional support for Israel is long-standing, broad, and deep, and monocausal interpretations are inadequate to explain Congress's special role. The rationale can be found in the public statements of members of Congress and extrapolated from their actions. Whatever their declared reasons for supporting Israel may be, they are undergirded by personal conviction. In this the Holocaust, Israel's role as a democratic ally, the Judeo-Christian heritage, and other similar factors play a part. These factors are reinforced by extensive and often close contacts with Israelis and their supporters and a knowledge of Israel and its problems derived from the media and similar sources. There is also a political basis for this support. Members of Congress worry about reelection and see Israel and its supporters as a component of that factor. Israel's supporters are active in campaigns and in fundraising and thus they can help reelection bids. Also, there is a generally held view that opposing Israel could lead to defeat at the polls — indeed, it is thought by some to be a form of political suicide. There is a general feeling that support for Israel is politically "cost free" and might well be a positive factor for an incumbent. The obverse is a threat, real or imagined, that if the member does not provide support there will be negative political consequences. The political argument is offered by those critical of U.S. policy, such as George Ball and James Abourezk, who attribute it largely to the existence of a large and influential U.S. Jewish lobby, which in their view exerts inordinate influence and perverts U.S. interests. This school suggests that the motivation for Congressional support can be found in the political and financial power of pro-Israel forces. This perspective has been fostered by some former members of Congress who attribute their defeat for reelection to the power of pro-Israel forces. They argue that Congress functions in response to the power of the lobby even when elections are not imminent.

Another factor contributing to Congressional support of, and the general sympathy for, Israel's position is the significant interaction between members of Congress and Israeli government officials and diplomats. Congressional delegations visit Israel frequently, and these official visits are supplemented by large numbers of official and nonofficial staff visits. Visits tend to generate understanding and support for Israel's position. These extended contacts add to the connections between the two states and reinforce the special connection between Congress and Israel.

The media is the dominant source of foreign policy information for the general public. Despite the disinterested accuracy of much of the reporting, the U.S. media is often brief and sometimes simplistic in its approach to foreign policy topics and in its presentation and analysis, especially on complex Middle Eastern issues. Television, a major source of information for the general public, allows little more than extended sound bites. What can be said that is meaningful about the U.S.-Israel relationship or the Arab-Israeli conflict in a segment of two to three minutes duration?

Public opinion affects Congressional decisions and interest groups gain influence when public opinion supports their positions. It is difficult to measure with precision, but the data provide reliable, if imperfect, indicators and snapshots of public thinking about a particular issue at a particular point. Public support for Israel has been strong and informed Americans consistently have been more willing to declare support and sympathy for Israel than for the Arab states and continue to endorse Israel's existence, integrity, and security.[6]

The U.S. moral commitment to a Jewish State in Palestine and, later, to Israel, was reflected in public opinion surveys conducted between 1946 and 1948 when an overwhelming majority of the American people supported Jewish immigration to Palestine and the creation of a Jewish state there. During this period, the Arabs garnered a greater share of the blame for the conflict in the region. Public opinion surveys after 1948 showed a high level of sympathy for Israel compared to the Arab states, and most Americans continued to have a positive image of Israel. Sympathy for Israel far outweighed that for the Arab cause. The public sympathy and support for the Jews and for the creation of a Jewish state focused on the image of a small and democratic state seeking to preserve its existence against hostile forces.

Sympathy for Israel has remained fairly constant over time, although there have been periods of increase (during and immediately after the 1967 and 1973 wars and in reaction to the completion of the Israeli withdrawal from Sinai in April 1982) and decrease (immediately after the Sabra and Shatilla massacres in 1982). It was sustained, with an occasional shift that soon reverted to its former position, through the 1970s and into the 1980s. Israel's attack on Iraq's Osirak reactor in June 1981, the attack on Palestine Liberation Organization (PLO) headquarters in Beirut in July 1981, the War in Lebanon in the summer of 1982, and the Sabra and Shatilla massacres in the fall of 1982 negatively affected Israel's image, but sympathy for Israel soon recovered despite a shift in its image as the "David" of the Middle East conflict. Throughout this period, Israel was seen in a mostly positive light because the Israeli government said it would go anywhere, anytime, to talk peace, while the Arabs refused to talk peace and engaged in war and terrorism against the Jewish state. This black and white image was occasionally blurred. Anwar Sadat's peace initiative altered it, if briefly and only with respect to him and Egypt. The intifada tarnished Israel's image as the world saw Israeli soldiers with guns chasing young kids armed with stones and the David-Goliath theme appeared to be turned on its head. PLO statements in the late 1980s suggesting a willingness to renounce terrorism, accept United Nations Security Council Resolutions 242 and 338, and accept Israel's right to exist contrasted with the Likud government's limitations on Israel's overall policy of going anywhere, anytime, to talk peace. All this further blurred the simple black and white image. Yet the depth and breadth of U.S. public support has made it resistant to serious erosion.

CAMPAIGN FINANCING AND THE POLITICAL ACTION COMMITTEES

U.S. politics are a function, to a large degree, of funding. Members of Congress and candidates for the presidency require huge sums of campaign money to get elected to public office. This fact of political life has particular relevance for the U.S.-Israel relationship.

The campaign finance reform laws, especially the Campaign Finance Act of 1974, had the effect of generating an explosive growth of PACs. PACs channel money to favored candidates on behalf of individuals who have reached their limits in direct contributions and on behalf of organizations and groups that were not permitted to contribute directly. PACs can also act independently and assist a candidate by working against an opponent, thereby assisting a preferred individual to whom it cannot contribute directly because of limits or other factors. Given the high level of political interest and activity in the Jewish community, it was inevitable that PACs would be created to represent its concerns. Generally, PACs are single issue in their orientation and most of the Jewish PACs are Israel-oriented. The first Jewish PACs were created in the late 1970s and now number about 100. While their contributions to political campaigns have grown at a very substantial rate and amount to millions of dollars, pro-Israel PACs still contribute less to political campaigns than corporate and trade union PACs.

Does PAC money generate the pro-Israel posture of the Congress? If all national election campaigns were federally funded so that political candidates never had to raise money, if there were no pro-Israel PACs, U.S. foreign policy and Congressional voting behavior would still be strongly pro-Israel for the reasons already discussed. There is no doubt, however, that the American Jewish community has used PACs effectively. American Jews have been active in campaigns and in securing and providing the funds for campaigns, again disproportionately to their size in the population as a whole. The American Jewish community has used the PACs to serve the political purposes of supporting preferred candidates. Among others, the number of PACs supporting Israel-oriented programs and candidates have grown in number. Much of the Israel-oriented PAC money is distributed based on the criterion of a candidate's position on Israel. As in other areas, Jewish political power focuses on the issue of Israel. The pro-Israel PACs have become large and distribute substantial funds to preferred candidates. Among the beneficiaries have been supporters of Israel such as Senator Bob Packwood and Senator Arlen Spector. Candidates who support pro-Israel positions can secure PAC funding, and those who are not friendly have such support withheld. Support can be garnered from across the nation to affect the outcome in a single state, and this message soon became clear in a number of prominent political races as high-profile candidates were defeated by the funding available through these sources.

POTENTIAL CHANGE

Given the changes in the international arena brought about by the end of the Cold War and the Gulf War, combined with concerns over the costs of various aid programs in a time of economic stress, is Congressional support for Israel in aid and related areas likely to diminish?

Because many of the elements that have conditioned support have not undergone serious change, the role of Congress in the special relationship is unlikely to be significantly modified in the near future despite alterations in the domestic, regional, and international spheres. The established pattern of Congressional assertiveness on matters affecting Israel is likely to continue. If a member bases support of Israel on a genuine belief in its right to exist as a secure state in the region because it is a democratic, like-image state, with a connection to the Judeo-Christian heritage, and perhaps fulfilling Biblical prophecy, it is unlikely that this view will be substantially affected by recent changes. On the contrary, it might well encourage further support in a world that has, in many respects, become more dangerous, particularly in Israel's neighborhood. Political factors might well be subject to alteration in the existing environment, but if members of Congress see support of Israel as directly connected, for whatever reason, to their political futures, major modifications in position are difficult to envisage. The public perception of Israel and of its Arab neighbors from which Israel traditionally has benefited has lost some of its luster because of questions about its leadership and policy during the Likud tenure, has again been modified in a positive direction during Rabin's tenure because of his general approach as well as progress toward peace in dealing with the PLO as well as several of the more moderate Arab states, especially Jordan.

The election of Bill Clinton in 1992 was widely interpreted to portend a greater focus on domestic economic and social issues. Nevertheless, foreign policy will not disappear and may preempt domestic concerns, especially in a crisis that cannot be ignored or deferred. This was especially apparent with the Hebron massacre in February 1994. Within the foreign policy environment, the Israel and Middle East factor has been fixed in the center for some time and is likely to sustain that position.

Alterations in the makeup of Congress in the 1992 and 1994 elections occasioned by departing members modified Congress's overall profile and this may affect the relationship. In the past it was argued that as the Congress became more politically conservative it might be less supportive of Israel's needs; however, this proved untrue during the 1980s. The relative youth of new members has led some to suggest that as the body's collective memory of World War II and the Holocaust grows dimmer and a "guilt" factor fades, support for Israel will decline. These younger members, who do not recollect Israel's origins, who have not witnessed the pioneering spirit of its people, who may not understand the trauma associated with the 1967 war, the argument goes, may prove less sympathetic toward Israel than their predecessors. Changes in committee leadership and composition may initially also lead to changes in attitude, as traditionally strong supporters of Israel depart from the scene; but, as in the past, such changes in the composition of Congressional committees will not necessarily lead to diminished support for Israel.

In the 1992 election some of Israel's staunchest friends (such as Congressmen Bill Green and Stephen Solarz of New York, Larry Smith of Florida, and Senator Robert Kasten of Wisconsin) retired or were defeated, as were some of Israel's traditional antagonists. Key Congressional committees include many traditionally pro-Israel members. Historically, the number of Jewish members of Congress has been approximately proportional to the Jewish population in the country, but this has changed in recent years. Although Jews constitute about 2.4 percent of the population, they hold 7.5 percent of House seats. In 1992, three Jews were elected to the incoming Senate class, bringing the total number of Jews in the Senate to ten. The number of Jews in the House of Representatives remained at 33, but included 11 new members. Of course, that these senators and representatives are Jewish is not an automatic guide to their views on Israel or on other issues that comprise the Jewish communal agenda. The new Jewish members of Congress come from more diverse geographical locations and backgrounds than their predecessors and they reflect the generational, geographic, and gender changes that are transforming American Jewry generally.

The size of the freshman Congressional class and its clear mandate for a focus on domestic issues required added effort by the pro-Israel lobby to establish relationships with new representatives and senators. The lobby must shift from an approach that emphasizes Israel's strategic military advantages to the United States to one that emphasizes the broad range of shared values and the economic advantages to be gained from continued foreign aid to Israel. Overall Congressional support for Israel is not likely to diminish if the lobby operates successfully and if the underlying ideological-emotional and political factors continue to exert their historical influence.

5

The Maturing of
Economic Relations

U.S.-Israel economic relations have been an outgrowth of the special political relationship between the two countries and not the result of purely economic factors. These ties have increased in magnitude and become more balanced over time, almost independent of changes in the political environment. The result is that U.S.-Israel economic relations today are quite different than they were at their outset 45 years ago.

Four types of exchanges dominate economic relations between the United States and Israel: financial assistance, trade in goods, investment flows, and technology exchanges. Recent developments in these four areas are presented in Table 5.1.[1] First, the data reveal that economic relations between the United States and Israel have intensified in recent years, growing from less than $1 billion in 1970 to almost $11 billion in 1990. There has been a trend toward increase in all four categories, particularly in commercial flows, which has not been affected by changes in political relations.

Official financial assistance to Israel has been the core of U.S.-Israel economic relations since the country was established in 1948. Initial modest aid flows have grown over the years to the current level of official assistance of $3 billion per year — $1.8 billion in military assistance and $1.2 billion in economic assistance. In 1992, in response to the significant economic burden Israel faced in absorbing an expected 1 million Jews from the former Soviet Union, the United States agreed to guarantee up to $10 billion over five years in commercial loans to Israel.

TABLE 5.1
U.S.-Israel Economic Relations: U.S. Financial
Assistance and Bilateral Trade and Investment
(in millions of US $)

	1960	1965	1970	1975	1980	1985	1990
U.S. Grants to Israel	13	5	13	507	1,025	3,350	2,987
U.S. Loans to Israel	43	60	81	271	760	0	0
U.S. Exports to Israel			430	999	1,549	1,679	2,726
U.S. Imports from Israel			186	308	954	2,138	3,489
U.S. Investment in Israel	NA	64	84	211	379	717	756
Israel Investment in U.S.	NA	NA	NA	NA	324	494	626
TOTAL			794	2,296	4,991	8,378	10,584

Given its magnitude, most of the attention paid to the bilateral economic relationship has focused on U.S. financial assistance, in spite of the fact that these relations have matured well beyond Israel's dependence on U.S. aid to a more balanced exchange between the two countries. Of the $5 billion in bilateral economic ties in 1980, over one third was loans and grants to Israel. During the 1980s the value of economic flows between the two countries doubled, and by 1991 the value of bilateral economic relations surpassed $12 billion. The emphasis of their economic relations also underwent changes during the decade, with financial assistance declining in importance from 36 percent of total bilateral flows in 1980 to 30 percent of those flows in 1991. Bilateral trade flows grew in importance over the same period, from 50 percent of the value of total economic exchanges in 1980 to 56 percent in 1991. Investment flows remained the smallest part of overall bilateral economic relations, although the value of the Israeli investment position in the United States doubled during the 1980s.

These changes in bilateral economic flows are the result of explicit efforts in both countries to deepen economic ties. Several significant developments took place during the 1980s to promote greater economic cooperation. In 1984 the United States agreed to restructure its financial assistance program by eliminating loans and providing Israel with grants. In 1985 the United States entered into a free trade agreement with Israel, which served as the precedent for the agreement with Canada and the subsequent North American Free Trade Agreement. In 1986, in support of Israel's emergency stabilization program, the United States provided $1.5 billion in supplemental assistance and set up a monitoring process for economic reform in Israel, the Joint Economic Development Group

(JEDG). In 1991 the United States increased its economic assistance for resettlement of Soviet Jews. This decade of closer economic ties ended with congressional approval of $10 billion commercial loan guarantees over five years to assist Israel absorb an expected 1 million Jewish refugees from the former Soviet Union.

The United States and Israel participate in an extensive set of technology exchanges. Three programs, the Binational Science Foundation (BSF), the Binational Industrial Research and Development (BIRD) fund, and the Binational Agriculture Research and Development (BARD) fund, were created with equal contributions by the United States and Israel. Their success has led to the establishment of a joint technology working group, announced during Prime Minister Rabin's visit to Washington in March 1993.

The original motivating forces behind U.S. financial assistance to Israel and the development of trade, investment, and technological cooperation are independent of one another. After 45 years, these economic ties constitute an important element in Israel's economy and in overall U.S.-Israel relations. Not only have these economic ties matured into a more balanced exchange, they also promise to strengthen relations between the United States and Israel in the post–Cold War era.

FINANCIAL ASSISTANCE

U.S. economic assistance to Israel began with small grants between 1952 and 1955 and expanded over the next ten years to include Export-Import, Food for Peace, and general economic loans. It was not until after the Six Day War in 1967 that the United States began providing Israel with military loans on an annual basis. These loans totaled $250 million through the 1960s. The 1973 Yom Kippur War served as another watershed for military assistance to Israel, beginning with $1.5 billion in military grants and almost $1 billion in military loans in 1974. Over the next ten years the United States provided $6.4 billion in military grants and $8.8 billion in military loans. In 1981 grants replaced loans for economic assistance and in 1984, when Israel faced the prospect of having to begin repaying past military loans, the United States also restructured its military assistance to Israel from loans to grants. Aid throughout the rest of the decade leveled off at $1.8 billion in military grants and $1.2 billion in economic grants annually.

Israel has been the recipient of the largest share of annual U.S. financial assistance since 1976.[2] Israel can use U.S. economic assistance funds, which until 1979 were focused on agricultural and food programs, with few conditions for general budgetary support. In 1987, Congress passed a provision allowing Israel, among others, to refinance its outstanding military debts carrying interest rates over 10 percent in the commercial market, guaranteed by the U.S. government. Israel currently owes the United States approximately $4.3 billion in direct economic and military loans, and another $5 billion in guaranteed commercial loans. The United States has never canceled any of Israel's official debts, but it has waived repayment of some loans as it has chosen to do periodically for others, such as Egypt.

The bulk of U.S. military aid to Israel is used to purchase military items produced in the United States. This is a clear case in which foreign aid creates jobs in the donor country. Given the amount of aid that never leaves the United States, the total amount of U.S. aid to Israel actually overstates its contribution to the Israeli economy. In fact, only a small percentage of U.S. military grants is spent in Israel itself, and most of the economic grant aid is devoted to servicing loans used to finance past weapon sales.

There has been growing concern on both sides about the level and nature of U.S. financial assistance to Israel. Foreign aid, regardless of the recipient, has never been popular in the United States, and it is becoming even more difficult to maintain Congressional support for a large foreign aid program, especially in light of pressures to cut domestic social spending. On the political side, it has been argued that the United States should use financial assistance to force Israel into making concessions to expedite the Middle East peace process. Israelis, on the other hand, have become increasingly concerned about their economy's dependence on the United States. Many observers believe that dependence on U.S. aid has diminished market incentives in the economy and has eroded the work ethic that helped build the country.

Since 1974 U.S. aid to Israel has been directly and indirectly linked to Israel's national security needs. Military grants have financed the vast majority of the increase in Israeli military spending over the period. Economic assistance has basically been tied to repaying the United States for military loans prior to 1984. The Cranston Amendment, which has been appended to foreign aid legislation since 1984, states that it is U.S. "policy and intention" to provide Israel with economic assistance "not less than" the amount it owes the United States in annual debt service payments (principal and interest). Although this provision is not binding, aid levels have conformed with its intent since 1984.

Given the economic and political realities of the day, and despite the favorable treatment Israel received from Washington throughout the

1980s, by the end of the decade Israeli officials realized that it would be unrealistic to depend on the United States to continue to meet all of Israel's economic needs. On the other hand, conditions in Ethiopia and reforms in the Soviet Union suggested that Israel had to be prepared to face huge financial burdens with absorbing significant numbers of new refugees. In addition, the government realized that it would need large amounts of foreign capital to help finance economic reforms that had been underway, albeit at a slow pace, since 1986. Based on these considerations the Israeli government decided in 1990 to request U.S. government guarantees for $10 billion in commercial loans over a five year period. It was clear that Israel needed access to more capital and the fact that these would be commercial loans would mollify those concerned about Israel's dependence on U.S. aid.

Israel's pursuit of loan guarantees was delayed by the Gulf War, and the Israeli government postponed making its official request until September 1991. President Bush asked Congress to delay consideration of Israel's request until January 1992, arguing that it would jeopardize his administration's efforts to bring the parties together for a Middle East peace conference. Following this delay the administration changed its position and conditioned its support for the loan guarantees on Israel's freezing of all settlement activity in the West Bank and the Gaza Strip.

Despite past avoidance of explicitly placing conditions on aid to Israel, the Bush administration was under pressure not to allow U.S. aid to be used to finance Israel's settlement activities in the West Bank and Gaza Strip. This pressure intensified with Israel's requests for assistance to absorb Ethiopian and Soviet Jewish refugees, as it was feared that these immigrants would be settled in the territories. Congress subsequently approved $400 million in housing loans and $5 million in refugee absorption funds, with the understanding that these funds would not be used in the territories.[3] This condition caused much tension between the Shamir government and the Bush administration. In the June 1992 Israeli election, Yitzhak Rabin and the Labor party assumed control of the Knesset and the government introduced a limited freeze on settlements in the territories. President Bush then announced that he would support loan guarantees for Israel, which he signed into law on October 6, 1992.[4]

The United States has played several different roles in providing financial assistance to Israel. Initially, the United States extended primarily humanitarian aid. Following the Six Day War, U.S. aid grew in size and nature, changing from purely humanitarian and economic assistance to include military assistance. During the 1980s the United

States took on another role, serving as Israel's "lender of last resort," providing emergency economic and humanitarian assistance and guaranteeing private loans. With the growing concern in the United States and Israel that aid distorts market incentives in the Israeli economy, Washington has taken an interest in promoting market-oriented reforms. Domestic budgetary pressures have also heightened interest in weaning Israel from current levels of U.S. aid. There seems to be agreement in Israel and the United States that large aid flows are not in either countries' long-run economic interests.

TRADE

Israel has been cut off from official commercial relations with its neighbors (except Egypt) as a result of the Arab boycott. Arab countries have refused to buy any products produced in Israel or made with inputs produced in Israel. Given its need to trade due to its lack of natural resources, Israel has followed a policy of securing access to European and American markets. In addition to providing economic certainty, commercial demands of these markets permitted Israel to move up the "industrial ladder," from selling agricultural goods to selling technology-intensive manufacturing goods.

The most important factor contributing to the increase in U.S.-Israel economic ties since 1984 is merchandise trade. Total bilateral trade between the two countries doubled from $3.4 billion in 1984 to $7.8 billion in 1992, accounting for more than half of all economic flows between Israel and the United States. Given the relative sizes of their two economies, this trade in aggregate is certainly more important to Israel than to the United States.

U.S. products have consistently made up approximately one-fifth of all Israeli imports. U.S. exports to Israel in 1992 were valued at $4 billion, of which half were concentrated in machinery and transport equipment, including aircraft and equipment, telecommunications equipment, automatic data processing machinery, and measuring and controlling instruments. The United States also has become an important market for Israeli goods. During the 1970s, the U.S. market accounted for less than 10 percent of Israeli exports; today it accounts for almost one-third of all Israeli exports.

The United States imported $3.8 billion in Israeli goods in 1992, almost all of which were manufacturing goods. At the top of the list were cut diamonds and jewelry, aircraft and equipment, telecommunications equipment, optical and medical equipment, parts for office machinery and automatic data processing machinery, and scientific and measuring instruments. The United States currently purchases 40 percent of Israel's machinery and mechanical appliances exports and over a third of Israel's optical, photographic, medical, and measuring devises exports.

Several political developments explain the expansion in U.S.-Israel trade in recent years. First and foremost, in 1985 the United States and Israel signed the Free Trade Area Agreement (FTA). Israel saw this as a means of locking in and expanding preferential access to the U.S. market, which it had been afforded under the Generalized System of Preferences. In addition to overarching political reasons, the United States saw this as an opportunity to ensure its own access to the Israeli market, as Israel had already signed a similar bilateral free trade agreement with the European Community in 1975. The FTA reduced tariffs in both countries and promoted more trade, but there is still no guarantee that both countries will reach the ultimate goal of complete duty-free bilateral trade by 1995.

Exchange rate stabilization and partial linking of the shekel to the dollar also helped stimulate trade flows. Between 1977 and 1986, the shekel moved relatively unincumbered against other currencies. Large budget deficits, financed primarily through monetary expansion, contributed to the rise in inflation and led to weak demand for the shekel. The weak shekel favored Israeli exporters but also raised the domestic price of imports. As part of the 1986 stabilization plan, the shekel was devalued, fixed to the value of the dollar, and then later pegged to a basket of currencies.

Using the exchange rate as an anchor helped stabilize the economy and renew the currency's credibility. This policy has not helped Israeli exporters, but it has brought down domestic prices of imports, contributing to bringing down overall inflation. Since the dollar plays an important role in the basket of currencies against which the shekel is valued, there is more stability in the shekel-dollar rate, which encourages more U.S.-Israel trade.

As with financial assistance, current trade patterns may not be a good indicator of future trade relations. Israel has been shifting its attention to two potential markets: the Far East and Eastern Europe and the former Soviet Union. Israel's heavy dependence on high technology industries makes the Far East a logical trading partner. The Arab boycott has long prevented these countries from fully developing trade relations with Israel, but the boycott now seems to be weakening. This market for Israeli goods should grow in importance as the boycott further weakens and Israel removes its import barriers.

Countries of Eastern Europe and the former Soviet Union are natural markets for Israeli products. Israel is now home to a high concentration of Eastern Europeans and former Soviets. These immigrants have technical skills to enhance Israeli exports and first hand knowledge of these markets. Israel's proximity to the region gives its exporters another advantage. Israel is already developing footholds in these countries, establishing both diplomatic and commercial ties. The major constraint on trade is the slow pace of economic development in the region.

Although U.S.-Israel trade promises to continue to be important, significant future growth in Israeli trade is most likely to be associated with these two emerging markets. Israeli trade policy has already shifted gears and is now focused on unilaterally removing import barriers to goods from countries other than the United States and throughout Europe. The initial excitement over the U.S.-Israel FTA has dissipated and neither country has shown much enthusiasm for negotiating the removal of tariffs on the most highly import-sensitive products. These negotiations were to begin in 1990 and tariff reductions were to be phased in by 1995. The United States and Israel have yet to agree on the list of products to be discussed, let alone any timetable for phasing out the tariffs. Initial interest in extending the original FTA to include trade in services has also faded as Washington has turned its attention to the North American Free Trade Agreement and the Uruguay Round of the General Agreement on Tariffs and Trade talks.

Trade is a primary example of how Israeli economic relations grew out of the political relationship and then took on a life of their own. The FTA, which was clearly motivated by political factors, opened the Israeli market to U.S. products, resulting in an almost doubling of U.S. exports to Israel between 1985 and 1992. And even though Israeli products already received preferential access to the U.S. market prior to the 1985 agreement, Israeli exports to the United States still grew by $2.3 billion between 1985 and 1992. Whatever the original political motivation for stimulating trade may have been, business interests will continue to follow markets. The newly opened markets in the United States and Israel are no exception.

FOREIGN INVESTMENT

Foreign investment is one aspect of the bilateral relationship that has not fully developed. The value of U.S. investment in Israel averaged about $600 million during the 1980s and has risen to more than $700 million over the last few years. In spite of Israel's policy to encourage foreign investment, there remain numerous barriers to foreign investment that explain the low investment. The most important barrier to foreign investment is the secondary Arab boycott. In addition to the direct boycott of Israeli products, the secondary boycott is aimed against any country that has commercial relations with Israel, including foreign investment. Israel's own national security concerns and restrictive bureaucratic business regulations have also deterred investment. There is growing awareness in Israel that the country needs foreign private capital in order to return to pre-1967 economic growth rates. Various governments have attempted to reduce these bureaucratic barriers since 1986. So far, the greatest achievement toward this goal has been reforms of Israel's capital market, including the removal of foreign capital controls. Economic stability since 1986 has also improved the investment environment in Israel.

However, the increase in foreign investment has not met the expectations of the Israeli government. It had hoped that foreign firms would significantly increase their investments in order to take advantage of Israel's preferential access in the European Community and U.S. markets. The combination of both agreements places Israel as the "bridge" between the two largest markets in the world. Given higher tariff walls between the United States and Europe, U.S. goods finished in Israel could enter the European market more easily than if they were shipped directly from the United States; the same would be true for European exports to the United States. But high transportation and labor costs and other investment barriers have prevented any serious development of this "bridge" trade through Israel.

The value of Israeli investment in the United States averaged $500 million during the 1980s and doubled to over $1 billion in 1991. Given the relative sizes of the two countries, it may appear surprising that Israeli investment in the United States has at times been larger than U.S. investment in Israel. One possible explanation for this is that U.S. barriers to foreign investment are much lower than those in Israel, thereby making it less costly for Israelis to invest in the United States than for Americans to invest in Israel. In addition, Israelis tend to view the United States as a safe place to invest while the converse is not necessarily true, although commercial investment in Israel may in fact have a higher economic return than investment in the United States. Overall, Israel is not an important player in foreign investment in the United States. Bilateral foreign direct investment flows are small in both absolute terms and relative to other U.S.-Israel economic flows.

TECHNICAL ASSISTANCE AND
TECHNOLOGY PARTNERSHIPS

Although the United States has been the largest donor of financial aid to Israel, it was not until 1986 when, in conjunction with providing $1.5 billion in supplemental assistance in support of the Emergency Stabilization Program in 1986, the United States began providing Israel with economic advice through the JEDG. Secretary of State George Schultz, an internationally recognized economist in his own right, personally supervised this effort to encourage Israel to introduce market-oriented reforms and begin the process of reducing its dependence on U.S. aid. Although the United States encourages econom-ic reforms in many countries, the extent of its involvement in promoting and monitoring economic reform in Israel is unique.

Both the U.S. and Israeli economies support technologically advanced industries. In the case of the United States, this is primarily the result of large investments in research and development; in Israel it is the result of a highly skilled labor force. Bilateral technological exchange is a natural outgrowth of these factors. This is one area in which economic relations between the United States and Israel can be characterized as cooperative and balanced, which is particularly noteworthy given the differences in the two countries' size and available resources.

The Israel-U.S. BIRD, founded in 1977, is at the center of the two countries' technological cooperation. With an original endowment of $110 million, equally financed by the United States and Israel, BIRD was established "to promote and support joint, non-defense, industrial research and development activities of mutual benefit to the private sectors of the two countries." Using the interest on the initial endowment, the Foundation provides matching funds to projects bringing together U.S. and Israeli companies for the purpose of developing and commercializing innovative, non-defense, high technology products or processes. Since its inception, BIRD has invested close to $100 million in over 300 projects, 175 of which have already led to more than $3 billion in sales. These projects have also produced five U.S. jobs for every one Israeli job created. About half of all new projects initiated within the last few years have been between companies brought together by BIRD. The Foundation is viewed by both the United States and Israel as a prime example of the benefits to be won by both countries when they enter into cooperative arrangements.

The BSF and the BARD are two additional examples of U.S.-Israel cooperation. Founded in 1972, BSF grants funds to support research in the natural and applied sciences, including agriculture, health sciences, and technologies of broad interest to both countries, such as mass transportation, energy, and environmental research. BARD, which was set up in 1977 with an endowment of $110 million, awards grants for cooperative research projects.

Building on these successes, on March 15, 1993, President Clinton and Prime Minister Rabin announced the establishment of a U.S.-Israel Science and Technology Commission, which is aimed at increasing cooperation in science, technology, and defense conversion programs. This new commission will encourage joint ventures in areas in which Israeli scientists, especially those from the former Soviet Union, have demonstrated expertise. The Commission has been named and the first set of meetings were held in Israel under the chairmanship of Commerce Secretary Ron Brown and Industry and Trade Minister Micha Harish.

THE INTERPLAY OF ECONOMIC AND POLITICAL RELATIONS

U.S.-Israel economic relations have undergone a transformation over the past decade. For the most part, economic relations have tended to track political relations between the two countries. In the early years of Israel's statehood, economic relations were dominated by humanitarian assistance from the U.S. government and private charity from the American Jewish community. By the mid 1960s the Israeli economy was being viewed as an economic miracle, and there was little fear of aid dependence or government ownership of enterprises. On the contrary, Israel's development from a primarily agricultural-based economy to technological leader was seen as a model to be emulated.

The Six Day War was a watershed in both political and economic terms. With its security burden heightened as a result of the war, Israel needed to maintain close political ties with arms-producing countries. From a purely economic standpoint, Israel's defense needs would have to be financed at home by either squeezing out expenditures on social programs or borrowing or printing more money to finance large budget deficits. Israel opted for both increased foreign borrowing abroad and looser economic policies at home as short-term solutions. Washington's heightened strategic interest in the region led the United States to provide much of the foreign capital to finance Israel's defense needs, first in the form of loans and later in the form of outright grants.[5]

A need for hard currency, in addition to its necessity to import all its raw material needs, intensified Israel's need to develop its export industries. As noted above, the Arab boycott had already cut off Israel's natural geographic market and threatened to go beyond. Faced with this prospect, Israeli exporters attempted to find markets in Europe and, to a lesser degree, in the United States. By the 1970s, Europe was Israel's primary commercial partner, providing markets for agricultural products, textiles, and manufactured goods, and the United States was Israel's strategic partner, providing financial and military assistance. The Yom Kippur War in 1973 reinforced this pattern. As a result of the war, the United States stepped up its military assistance to Israel.

American public opinion saw Israel first as the nation born out of the ashes of the Holocaust and later as the David surrounded by Goliaths and supported aid to Israel, in spite of its growth in magnitude and shift from humanitarian to military assistance. Israel now joined other "strategic" allies like Greece, Turkey, and Pakistan, and soon became the largest recipient of foreign aid. Israel seemed exempt from the American public's general reluctance to support foreign aid.

The enormous defense burden began to take its toll on Israel's domestic economy, however, which was already weighed down by the many state institutions designed to protect individual citizens' standard of living. To those who took a longer-term perspective, it was obvious that Israel was not going to be able to maintain these social programs while spending a large share of its GDP on meeting its security needs. The defense burden was already being financed by foreign borrowing, primarily from the United States, and growing inflation resulting from lax monetary policies at home. The first warning of trouble came in the early 1980s, when Israel was scheduled to begin making payments on the large military assistance loans made during and after the 1973 war. This was during the Reagan-Shamir era, a period of particularly close relations between the two countries. The United States responded to Israel's plight by converting many of its loans into outright grants.

Given the degree of overlap in strategic interests, there was never any serious threat of the United States conditioning economic assistance to Israel on achieving certain political objectives. But by the late 1970s, U.S. aid to Israel had grown from modest amounts of humanitarian aid to rather significant amounts of military and economic grants. In 1979, Washington pledged increased aid as an incentive for Israel and Egypt to sign the Egypt-Israel Peace Treaty. The United States basically financed the terms of the agreement.

The closer political ties between the United States and Israel that developed in the early 1980s contributed to increased economic ties between the two countries. Technological cooperation programs were initiated and Israeli products began to find their way into the U.S. market. In order to "level the playing field," the United States and Israel entered into negotiations to establish a free trade agreement. Their economic relations were beginning to shift from aid to trade, from official to commercial exchanges. The United States was becoming Israel's strategic and commercial partner.

The shift from loans to grants and the refinancing of outstanding loans came too late to counter misguided economic policies in Israel. By 1986, inflation was on its way to reaching 1,000 percent, and the central bank was hemorrhaging its foreign currency reserves. As it had consistently done when facing threats to its national security, Israel turned to the United States for assistance. Some rationalized this move by arguing that Israel's economic situation partially resulted from its significant defense burden, which the United States supported as part of its strategic interests in the region.

At the same time, U.S.-Israel political and economic relations, which had closely paralleled each other since 1967, began to diverge. On the one hand, Israel's strategic value to the United States appreciated during the Reagan administration. The resulting intensification of diplomatic relations was also expressed through economic means, with the conversion of loans to grants and the signing of a bilateral free trade agreement. On the other hand, shifts in U.S. public opinion, particularly as a result of the Lebanon War and the intifada, led to moderate pressure on Washington to place conditions on aid to Israel at the same time that this aid was growing. Israelis began to be concerned over their ability to service the country's outstanding debt to the United States. Economists and policymakers also began raising questions over Israel's dependence on U.S. aid, and its impact on the structure of the economy.

The nature of U.S.-Israel economic relations was transformed as a result of these factors. The test came in 1986, when the Israeli economy was facing collapse. In response to requests for financial assistance, the United States agreed to provide to stabilize the currency instead of additional loans or grants. In direct exchange for this, Israel agreed to the establishment of the JEDG, through which the U.S. government hoped to encourage Israel to institute responsible domestic economic policies. This was the first time that the United States placed conditions, albeit loose ones, on financial assistance to Israel, and also the first time that the United States attempted to outright influence economic policies in Israel.

The new free trade agreement and changes in macroeconomic factors led to a significant expansion in private commercial relations between the two countries. Trade began to grow at a much faster rate than aid, and official economic flows began to give way to private commercial flows. Along with this growth in bilateral trade, however, came disagreements over trade practices, as industrialists and workers in trade-sensitive industries began to have a voice in the U.S.-Israel economic relationship.

The expansion of economic relations to include trade provided another target for Israel's adversaries. In 1988, for example, under a new condition placed on the Generalized System of Preferences program, a complaint was filed against Israel for unfair labor practices in the territories. The complaint was later dismissed, but it set a precedent for using U.S.-Israel economic relations as means for political attacks.

The culmination of this decade of change came with Israel's request for $10 billion in loan guarantees. It had become clear to Israeli policymakers that the country needed to attract large amounts of foreign capital in order to support market-oriented reforms initiated in 1986. The arrival of thousands of Ethiopian refugees and the prospect of up to 1 million Soviet Jewish immigrants had intensified this need for foreign capital. By this time, however, Israeli policymakers were becoming more sensitive to the potential deleterious effects of direct economic grants on the Israeli economy. This, combined with U.S. budgetary constraints and a shift in U.S. public opinion, led the Israeli government to request that the United States provide assistance through guaranteeing private loans.

At the same time that the Israeli economy was under pressure to absorb the daily arrival of thousands of Soviet immigrants, the United States was pushing hard to convene an international peace conference. Arab nations argued that by providing the loan guarantees the United States would prejudice the outcome of the meetings, and they called on Washington to withhold the guarantees until Israel agreed to stop its settlement activities in the territories. In the end, the Arab states and the Bush administration prevailed: the United States delayed agreement on the loan guarantees in spite of strong Congressional support for Israel, and Israel agreed to participate in the Madrid peace conference, which was convened in October 1991. Yitzhak Shamir's Likud party lost in the national elections in June 1992 — in which economic and security issues played determining roles — and the Bush administration subsequently agreed to provide the loan guarantees, but only after the new Rabin government curtailed settlement activity in the territories.

This episode is important in the context of the bilateral economic relationship for two reasons. First, the loan guarantees introduced a new form of market-oriented economic assistance with lower budgetary outlays. Second, this episode demonstrated a willingness on the part of the United States to allow economic assistance to be used as an overt means of achieving its political objectives. In the case of emergency aid in 1986, U.S. economic assistance was conditioned on meeting economic objectives, that is, introducing market-oriented reforms. In this case, granting the loan guarantees was directly conditioned on changing Israel's settlement policy. While it is common practice for the United States to place conditions on its aid, it is rare for these conditions to be so specific, especially in the case of Israel. This episode serves as the transition into the next era of economic relations between the United States and Israel.

THE FUTURE OUTLOOK

U.S.-Israel economic relations have matured through several stages. Initially, the United States provided Israel with humanitarian aid and the weapons to defend itself from its enemies. As political relations between the two countries deepened, so did economic relations. In the decade after the 1973 war, U.S. military assistance grew rather substantially and economic assistance, primarily to finance Israel's defense capabilities, followed not far behind. U.S.-Israel economic relations were driven by political considerations during the 1980s. Even as the strategic relationship between the two countries deepened, periodic tensions erupted. Both countries pursued the common objective of Israeli economic independence through expanded commercial trade and investment flows. But Israel's economy was not yet ready to stand on its own, and on several occasions Israel turned to the United States for economic assistance and support.

The nature of U.S. assistance to Israel is maturing together with overall U.S.-Israel relations. The use of direct grants is shifting to a reliance on guarantees of private loans. Aid dependence is changing to trade interdependence. Strategic interests have expanded to include encouraging market-oriented economic reforms in Israel. Cooperation in technology is growing between the two countries. Overall, economic relations are shifting from one-sided to more balanced exchanges.

A slow process of weaning Israel from U.S. assistance has begun. The level of military and economic grants to Israel has not kept pace with Israeli (or U.S.) inflation since 1987. Budgetary constraints and weakening public opinion suggest that U.S. foreign aid to the region will most likely undergo some changes over the coming years. Unlike the period following the signing of the Camp David Accords, a decline in assistance to Israel and Egypt is likely to occur, in spite of increased defense demands to secure any peace that might evolve from the current talks.

Economic investment will probably replace military hardware as a means of "buying friends" in the region. But the diplomatic efforts to date between the United States and Israel have been slow to produce significant increases in trade and investment in Israel. The U.S. government should encourage private initiatives in Israel in order to shift its role from the constantly nurturing parent to that of the friendly local bank, assisting Israel in making investments which are consistent with its long-term economic interests.

The most important economic development in Israel over the last few years is the arrival of approximately half a million immigrants from the former Soviet Union. These immigrants represent the greatest migration of highly skilled human capital in the twentieth century. They present Israel with immediate absorption costs, but the challenge facing Israel is how to turn this burden into an economic boom. The United States and Israel should explore ways of exploiting this influx of brain-power for the benefit of the Israeli economy through joint innovation and commercialization projects. U.S. capital, immigrant brain-power, and Israeli access to the European and U.S. markets should combine to produce benefits for all parties.

Israel's recent achievements in gaining virtually world-wide diplomatic recognition will contribute to its efforts to expand its economic relations outside of the United States and Europe. Japan's willingness to invest resources in the Middle East may be another test of its commitment to the post–Cold War alliance. Its agreement to become involved in the multilateral peace negotiations and chairing the sessions on environmental issues is just the beginning of this process. The United States should play an active role in encouraging others to invest economic resources in the region.

One of the most important steps the United States can take to assist Israel's move toward economic independence is to work for the complete removal of the Arab boycott. Such a development should not be expected to lead to a significant increase in Israeli trade, because Israel is now entrenched in the European and American markets and has little interest in developing less prosperous regional markets. Lifting the boycott should lead, however, to increased foreign investment in Israel, which would, in turn, promote market-oriented reforms and further reduce Israel's dependence on foreign assistance. The Arab boycott has also had the perverse effect of discriminating against Palestinian products. Lifting the boycott should open a safety valve by enabling Palestinians to export their products to nearby markets, starting the process of helping Palestinians become more economically independent and possibly easing Palestinian-Israeli tensions.

As U.S.-Israel relations continue to mature, Israel must internalize the reality of economic separation from the United States. Economic reforms are moving Israel in the right direction, but the notion that the United States will also be there to help has taken away some of the urgency behind these reforms. Israeli leaders must pay more attention to the short-term and long-term economic costs of their choices, and explain these costs to their constituents. Reducing aid levels is not the answer to Israel's economic problems. The United States, while continuing to provide economic support, should help make the cost of such aid more transparent and encourage Israel to undertake constructive policies today as an investment in its future economic security.

Much of the aid that currently goes to Israel is being used to finance yesterday's military purchases, which the United States encouraged as part of its strategic interests in the region. If the United States were to reduce aid flows abruptly, leaving Israel with the bill for these purchases, this would not only prove disastrous to the Israeli economy but it would undermine Washington's attempts to build alliances after the end of the Cold War. The move from aid to loan guarantees seems an appropriate first step in helping wean Israel from U.S. financial assistance. The next five years should reveal whether this kind of assistance is adequate.

Although there is general agreement that it is in the long-term interest of the Israeli economy to reduce its dependence on foreign aid, continued U.S. assistance is necessary because of previous commitments between the two countries. Because the United States cannot easily forgive official Israeli debt, and Israel cannot pay this debt without help, there are few options available for reducing Israeli aid dependence. One possibility would be for the United States to forgo payment of interest on outstanding loans and request repayment of principle only.

Another option would be for Israel to privately refinance the remaining portion of its military loans under the 1987 Congressional provision. The U.S. government might also assist Israel in refinancing all of these loans to take advantage of lower interest rates and Israel's improved credit rating. A more creative option would be to explicitly link repayment of U.S. loans to increased trade from Israel. The United States might agree to allow Israel to use the funds earmarked for debt service to provide credits to Israeli exporters. This would certainly raise concern among import-competing industries in the United States, but it would help wean Israel from U.S. aid while promoting economic activity in Israel.

As economic relations between the United States and Israel have broadened, so too has the interest in economic issues. The creation of the JEDG in 1986 is evidence that the United States is concerned about long-term developments in the Israeli economy itself. Unfortunately, the activities of the JEDG have fallen off rather substantially since the group's initial involvement in the Israeli stabilization program. The JEDG has the potential of serving as the primary vehicle to exchange information, discuss policy options, and address economic grievances. Israel has gotten used to solving many of its economic problems outside traditional avenues and through political channels, sidestepping those institutions which may be better suited for dealing with such issues. Both countries should renew their commitment to the JEDG and agree to look for ways to use this institution to their mutual benefit. A reinvigorated JEDG should begin negotiations on the most import-sensitive goods and fully implement the outstanding provisions of the U.S.-Israel Free Trade Area Agreement.

U.S.-Israel economic relations grew out of the special relationship that exists between the two countries. Economic relations between the two countries began as one-sided, with the United States providing Israel with financial assistance. Over time both the size and nature of economic exchanges between the United States and Israel have changed. Economic relations are now more balanced, with the addition of trade, investment, and technological cooperation to U.S. financial assistance to Israel. The nature of U.S. aid to Israel is also changing, taking into account the long-term interests of the Israeli economy and a different budgetary environment in the United States. These developments will form the foundation for the next stage of economic relations between the United States and Israel.

6

Policy Parameters

Israel and the Middle East will continue to command the attention of United States policymakers into the twenty-first century, despite the end of the Cold War and the current introspective focus on domestic matters. Before the creation of the Soviet Union, the region was important because of its connection to Western civilization, its geostrategic location, and its natural resources; it retains that significance after the end of the USSR. Israel is not "like any other country," and the particulars of its history that earned it a special place in the American consciousness continue to resonate in the American mind.

The end of the Cold War and the adversarial superpower relationship have left the United States without a compelling national security threat and clearly identified purpose. The Middle East benefits, in the short term, from the outcome of the Cold War and the fact that it is no longer a focal point of East-West conflict, as well as from the outcome of the Gulf War. Nevertheless, a peaceful Middle East is unlikely in the 1990s. The dominant regional conflict between Israel and the Arabs has taken a positive turn with the Madrid-inaugurated peace process, and especially the Israel-Palestine Liberation Organization (PLO) Declaration of Principles (DOP), the Washington Declaration, the Israel-Jordan Peace Treaty, and attendant negotiations, but short-term comprehensive solutions remain elusive. Even if this conflict is resolved, implementing the solution will take years, and the region has numerous other disputes, along with problems of internal turmoil, that pose dilemmas for regional leaders as well as challenges for the United States.

United States interests in the Middle East were relatively constant between World War II and the end of the Cold War. The central concern was to limit Soviet influence, prevent Soviet predominance or hegemony, and avoid conflict — conventional and nuclear — with it. The United States also attempted to end the Arab-Israeli conflict, to secure the survival, security, and well-being of Israel, and to ensure the stability of friendly Arab regimes. Washington sought to ensure the reliable flow of Middle Eastern oil to its friends and its allies and, later, to the United States, at reasonable prices. Earlier in the century, U.S. companies developed an economic interest in the region's oil industry and, more recently, the U.S. government tried to secure the investment of oil revenues in the United States and access to the region's markets for U.S. goods and services. Washington tried to limit arms supply to the region to maintain the military balance and thus to prevent conflict but, over time, it also became an important, if not a dominant, purveyor of arms and related military services.

United States interests in the next decade will include both traditional elements and newer concerns. The region will be increasingly important in international oil markets because of its vast proven reserves, productive capacity, and export capability. Middle Eastern oil is significant for U.S. business and financial interests, and it is also of increasing strategic importance to the United States. There is a concomitant U.S. interest in access to the region's markets and its financial resources. Washington seeks to sustain and improve relations with moderate Arab states and to prompt their movement toward the adoption of democratic processes. The special relationship with Israel as a democratic, stable, and progressive state in the region retains its centrality even as Israel's strategic utility diminishes without a threat comparable to that formerly posed by the Soviet Union. The Middle East is the cradle of Western civilization and of the monotheistic traditions; the organizing ideas of the Western world draw inspiration from and sustain interest in the area. The Judeo-Christian heritage and its manifestations animate policy, as will other shared values.

PURSUE PEACE AND ASSURE ISRAEL'S SECURITY

The pursuit of an Arab-Israeli peace has been, and must continue to be, a major foreign policy concern for a U.S. president.

The end of the Cold War and the success of the U.S.-led coalition against Iraq in the Gulf War did not end the threat to U.S. interests in the region. The prime U.S. objective remains the creation of a secure and stable Middle East, from which oil flows reliably to the United States and its friends and allies at a reasonable price, and in which a secure Israel lives at peace and maintains normal relations with moderate and stable (and increasingly democratic) Arab neighbors. Optimally, war would cease to be an instrument of national policy, and sophisticated conventional and non-conventional weapons systems would no longer be necessary components of the defense strategies of the regional states. But this is not a viable short-term outcome and, therefore, policy must concentrate on intermediate stages.

The United States must therefore sustain Israel's ability to deter Arab-Iranian military threats and to defend itself in the event of an attack, so that U.S. troops will not be required to secure Israel's survival and security, as they were in the case of Kuwait. To achieve these ends the United States must continue to provide Israel with adequate quantities of advanced military equipment to sustain Israel's "qualitative edge" over potential adversaries.

To facilitate the movement to peace and to assure Israel's security and survival in the interim, the United States should clearly reiterate its ultimate specific objectives in the peace process as well as its commitment to Israel's survival and security. This will help avoid Arab misunderstanding of the U.S. position and will reinforce Israeli confidence in its position and in its relationship with the United States, facilitating concessions necessary for progress in the peace process.

The United States and Israel see the nature of an Arab-Israeli peace in similar terms, even while they disagree on some specific elements of the peacemaking process and some of the specific solutions. Both see peace as more than just the absence of war. It is defined as real, lasting, just, and comprehensive, and is based on United Nations Security Council Resolutions 242 and 338. It must be achieved by direct negotiations between Israel and its Arab neighbors. There must be enduring treaties, normalized relationships, and real reconciliation between the parties, secured through a wide-ranging set of irreversible associations including diplomatic links, open borders, commerce, and tourism.

No comprehensive peace will be achieved unless the U.S. commitment to Israel's existence and security is clear to Israel and the Arabs. Although the Arabs know and understand the nature of the special relationship and the commitment, periodically some choose to misinterpret or test it. The U.S.-Israel contretemps over U.S. loan guarantees in 1991 and 1992 was of limited long-term value in progressing toward an Arab-Israeli peace and regional stability, but it had short-term negative effects. Israelis, unsure of United States support, became hesitant about entering into negotiations, while Arabs were convinced that they needed to make few concessions to Israel given the deteriorating U.S.-Israel relationship.

Over the years, despite the substantial links that have developed between the United States and Israel, the widespread belief in the existence of a commitment, and the assurances contained in agreements such as the Sinai II accords and the Egypt-Israel Peace Treaty, the nature, form, and content of the United States commitment to Israel has remained imprecise. Even though the United States and Israel have signed a number of specific, formal, bilateral agreements covering a wide range of subject areas — including agriculture, economics, oil supply, economic assistance, educational exchange, science and technology, and security and defense — these do not articulate the overarching commitment. Although it is commonly assumed that the United States would come to Israel's assistance should it be gravely threatened, assurances to this effect may be necessary, especially after the Scud missile attacks on Israel during the Gulf War.

A U.S. guarantee for Israel's security is not a new idea, but it has found new arguments and supporters after the Gulf War. The existence of such a guarantee would serve as a deterrent to potential aggressors. If, within its terms, the pledge to assure Israel's qualitative edge is institutionalized, the danger of misperception and potential conflict would be reduced. The commitment need not be incorporated in a formal treaty or similar document that would, in any event, be interpreted or reinterpreted at each juncture. It could take the form of clear presidential pronouncements endorsed by Congressional resolution. The value of the commitment will be in the willingness to undertake it, and in U.S. sincerity to implement it, if challenged. This is a function of the decision makers, the particular challenge, and the relationship on which it is based. The cost of the commitment to the United States lies in its implementation, and that might never be formally tested.

In recent years Israelis have expressed mixed views concerning a formal treaty relationship with the United States, although they recognize the value of a restated commitment and strategic connection. They worry, among other things, that such an agreement might impose limitations on Israel's freedom of action in matters relating to its defense. In any case, Israel does not seek the involvement of U.S. military personnel in its efforts to meet its security requirements; it continues to believe in self-reliance, despite the Patriot missile episode during the Gulf War. But it does want U.S. reassurances that it will be able to sustain its qualitative edge over its Arab and other potential adversaries, and that it can secure the military equipment essential for its security so long as the potential for hostilities exists. This will help to convince Israel that it may safely make concessions to its adversaries in the peacemaking process.

U.S. economic and military aid has not only helped Israel to ensure its security, it has helped to bridge the gap between the parties in negotiations and has been effective in inducing Israeli concessions, as in the Sinai II accords and the Egypt-Israel Peace Treaty. In the latter instance, Israel's agreement to withdraw from the Etam and Etzion air bases in the Sinai Peninsula was closely linked to the United States pledge to assist in the construction of new and sophisticated air bases in Israel's Negev. The U.S. commitment to meet Israel's oil needs, if alternative sources were not available, facilitated Israel's decisions to withdraw from the area of the Sinai oil fields. U.S. guarantees of the basic treaty were important inducements to both Israel and Egypt.

Confidence between the partners is essential for the relationship to flourish and progress toward Arab-Israeli peace, as only a confident Israel will take risks in the peace process. Maintaining confidence and reestablishing it where it had been eroded is essential. Official Israeli behavior suggests the value of reliable reassurances by the United States, despite the argument by some that they are unnecessary. Measures that reduce confidence are counterproductive and are likely to be self-defeating. Israel's history suggests that the establishment of peace, and its taking risks and making concessions, is closely linked to its feeling of security and its confidence in its situation and the United States as an ally and guarantor of the process. Israel responds positively when it is confident and reassured, not under pressure, as illustrated by the role of the United States in securing the Egypt-Israel Peace Treaty and as an intermediary in the Madrid peace process. This assumes the continued congruence of U.S. and Israeli policy to achieve peace. Encouraging Israel to adopt policies or procedures that will advance the peace-making process continues to be an appropriate element in the bilateral dialogue, even while avoiding the substitution of U.S. solutions and judgments for Israeli decisions. Seeking to impose these will continue to be improper and prove counterproductive. The counterargument focuses on pressuring Israel to make peace and the concessions necessary to bring it about by cutting U.S. economic and military aid as well as broader support. The argument is that Israelis seek this pressure to have a rationale for doing what might otherwise be politically unthinkable. Despite the apparent logic of these suggestions, they have not been employed with success in the bilateral relationship — on matters of crucial centrality, reassurance has been, and will continue to be, the effective mechanism.

Will Israel regard United States reassurances as reliable? Although the record is mixed, Israel has sought reassurances as a mechanism to allow it a greater margin of security and to help it to accept regional political changes. Not all Israelis will agree on what constitutes a reaffirmation of the U.S. commitment or its reliability. Even in the best of circumstances, small states tend to be wary of the actions of larger powers and harbor suspicions about the policies and actions of even their best friends and allies. Although there will be suspicions about U.S. motives and questions about U.S. reliability, the preferred avenue is to provide the reassurances in the expectation that they will help to convince Israel of the solidity of its position and of the prospects for the ultimate success of its venture.

Confidence often has been a function of close and continuous consultation between the United States and Israel. The need for its continuation is both obvious and critical. In the past, the absence of such consultations has led to tensions that prevented the achievement of desired objectives. In the absence of Arab interlocutors, however, the United States and Israel should not engage in negotiations with each other, especially when they disagree on the process or specific policies. The two states should consult concerning the peace process, thereby avoiding the recriminations that arise from unilateral actions. This was apparent in the Reagan plan of 1982, which was presented to Israel's government without warning or consultation although Jordan's King Hussein had been informed, a factor that contributed to Begin's rejection of the plan and the decision to annex the Golan Heights. Similarly, relations suffered as a result of Israel's unilateral decision to bomb the Iraqi nuclear reactor in 1981 and invade Lebanon in 1982.

THE ROLE OF THE UNITED STATES: HONEST BROKER AND GUARANTOR

The United States must continue to press for peace in the Middle East, focusing on the Arab-Israeli dispute. The United States will continue to be the dominant power with the ability to serve as a facilitator of the peace process (despite occasional but circumscribed roles for smaller powers such as Norway in 1993) and, therefore, it must continue to inspire the confidence of all potential participants — but it need not do so at the expense of its own interests and principles. As a full partner in the process, the United States should continue to make clear its opposition to groups whose goals are to subvert the peace process and who engage in terrorism and other violence to achieve that end. The U.S. role in peacemaking must be that of an honest broker engaged in achieving full-faith negotiations between the parties whose outcome has not been predetermined. Washington should not seek to impose its own will by forcing unilateral concessions from the parties. It should serve as a valued and valuable intermediary seeking to narrow the differences and bridge the gaps between the parties. It should not be a substitute for the interlocutors, who can reach a meaningful, comprehensive, just, and lasting peace only if they are the parties to the process. Facilitation and assistance should not give way to substitution; the mechanism for peace must be direct talks between Israel and its Arab interlocutors.

The United States emerged as the central external power in the search for a solution to the Arab-Israeli conflict in the wake of the Yom Kippur War and especially after the Gulf War. Its successes in the 1970s, and with the more recent Madrid conference process, were based on an indispensable combination of increasingly multifaceted relations with the Arab states and on continued traditional linkages with Israel. For the Arab actors (including the Palestinians), there is no alternative except to cooperate with the United States. Despite their criticism of its policies, they recognize that the United States is the only power capable of achieving the preferred policy outcomes. They recognize the relative power and weight of the United States because it is a superpower and because of its connection to Israel. They invoke and seek to repeat the policies of President Eisenhower in 1956–57 during the Suez crisis and of President Bush in 1991–92 on the loan guarantee issue. Anwar Sadat turned to Washington to support his initiative that eventually led to the Egypt-Israel Peace Treaty in 1979 and the PLO sought a dialogue with the United States in the 1980s, despite the availability of the Soviet Union as an alternative.

The United States is the only power able to pursue a major role to resolve the Arab-Israeli conflict and is likely to sustain this solitude, despite recent growing assertiveness by Russia. Nevertheless, and despite its crucial role and achievements, the United States has never been neutral concerning the outcome of the Arab-Israeli conflict and the future of Israel. It has been and is an honest broker in the Arab-Israeli peace process, but one with a "bottom line," because it is not disinterested, nor indifferent, nor can it be. Although it can be argued that the United States should be circumspect and evenhanded in its approach, its position concerning Israel's future is clear and well known. The United States vision of peace in the Middle East incorporates an Israel living in a normal relationship with its neighbors as an accepted, legitimate member of both the international and Middle Eastern communities. It believes that Jerusalem should not be redivided, as it was from 1949 to 1967, and that its status should be the outcome of direct negotiations rather than of the unilateral actions of one party or another. Secure and recognized borders between the parties should reflect a negotiated outcome, not U.S. preferences or dictates, although it envisages some insubstantial alterations in the 1949–67 armistice lines.

The firmness of a U.S. position, once adopted, plays a valuable role. The U.S. position concerning a dialogue with the PLO, adopted in the 1970s and maintained with remarkable tenacity over the ensuing period, through several administrations and in the face of numerous challenges, ultimately led the PLO to modify its position on central issues and to the dialogue initiated in Oslo and continued after the signing of the DOP.

In addition to its role as an honest broker, the United States can serve as a potential guarantor of the peace. The role it played with regard to the Sinai II arrangement is a useful precedent. The U.S. presence was indispensable, albeit small and circumscribed in scope. U.S. monitors in the Sinai Peninsula permitted Israel and Egypt to disengage their forces and permitted critical first steps toward accommodation and an overall settlement. This might be a useful precedent with regard to the Golan Heights. Sinai II clearly engaged U.S. prestige, participation, and expenditure in the continued search for an Arab-Israeli peace. The United States was the only state with the standing to achieve such an agreement, and the only one that could provide the economic, military, and political commitments and assurances essential for its maintenance.

There was concern on the part of Congress, the media, and the American public that placing U.S. personnel in the Sinai Peninsula between the opposing forces would lead to direct U.S. involvement in the conflict in the event the peace broke down. Such concerns would probably arise again if U.S. troops were deployed between opposing forces in the Golan Heights, the West Bank, the Gaza Strip, or between Israel and Lebanon where, unlike in the Sinai, the distances between the sides are small. Would it be a trip wire by which U.S. casualties might lead to U.S. participation in conflict? There is the specter of the "advisers in Vietnam" analogy with the potential for a growth in U.S. involvement, but the counterargument suggests a flawed analogy — in the case of Sinai the U.S. presence was minimal in size, was desired by both parties, and could be withdrawn if there was an outbreak of hostilities. Despite a lengthy presence there were no significant incidents, and the United States was not drawn into combat. The force served its intended purpose.

As with the successful Sinai deployment, a U.S. presence in any of these areas could be circumscribed to minimize potential dangers. In Sinai II there were not more than 200 technically skilled U.S. civilians assigned to monitor functions. They served in a delimited zone between the two parties that had agreed to refrain from hostilities. Although others could perform the technical intelligence functions, the United States' presence had a broader symbolic purpose that could not be served by other parties, and was sought by both Israel and Egypt.

A further parallel is to be found in the Multinational Force and Observers — an effective, low-profile, peacekeeping operation placed on the Sinai Peninsula between Egypt and Israel, whose origins are in the Egypt-Israel Peace Treaty of 1979. The treaty called for the withdrawal from the peninsula of Israel's civilian and military assets by 1982 and the return of the territory to Egypt in a series of phased Israeli withdrawals and Egyptian advances. The peninsula was divided into a number of zones, and the number and types of military equipment in each was specified. The treaty called for United Nations forces to monitor and verify treaty compliance and implement the security arrangements, but Arab and Soviet opposition prevented the Security Council from authorizing the appropriate observers. This led the United States, Egypt, and Israel to create the Multinational Force and Observers. An August 1981 protocol codified it as the replacement of the United Nations. It is an operation stationing U.S. troops as well as civilian observers (as in the 1975 arrangement) in a troubled area. The United States was the only national contingent specified in the protocol. The force is composed of some 3,000 military and civilian personnel from 11 countries and began operations in April 1982. It is only lightly armed for self-defense and cannot perform offensive operations. Its mission is to monitor treaty compliance and reduce the likelihood of surprise attack; neither its mission nor its equipment permits it to engage a major force from either party. The United States also manages the essential logistical network for its operations.

CONSENSUS AND DISCORD

The expectation that any alliance or special relationship should be marked by a wholly congruent and symmetric set of positions and policies is unrealistic. Friction is a component of relationships, even among close allies. Strains between the United States and Israel have parallels in the United State' relationships with its North Atlantic Treaty Organization allies and other states with which it has formal treaties of alliance. In recent years, the United States has had notable and high profile clashes over political and economic issues with Canada, Japan, Germany, France, and the European Community. It has engaged in sometimes acrimonious debate on defense burden-sharing and other strategic issues with both the North Atlantic Treaty Organization and Japan. At times, its friends and allies have opposed U.S. initiatives, such as the reflagging of ships in the Persian Gulf, the air raid against Libya, and actions concerning Bosnia.

The differences between the United States and Israel, however, are akin to those within a family: they focus on tactics and policy, but not on fundamentals. The special relationship has been replete with broad areas of agreement and numerous examples of discord over more than four decades. Broad agreement, understanding, and a generalized commitment to peace exist, and specific questions and issues have been approached within that framework. It is concerning specifics that the relationship often has had its episodes of disagreement and that each has been active in its efforts to influence the actions of the other. The two states maintain general accord on interests and broad policy goals — including the need to prevent war, the need to resolve the Arab-Israeli conflict, and the need to sustain Israel's survival and security. However, as the bilateral dialogue has increasingly dealt with details, there have been disturbances, sometimes serious, in the relationship. Strains are inevitable given the extensive nature of the issues considered in the dialogue.

The linkage of the United States and Israel reached new positive levels after 1967, when there was an exclusivity in the relationship as a result of the Six Day War, the ruptures of relations between the United States and some Arab states, the general concord on the need for and content of a settlement, and the intrusion of the Soviet Union. However, this exclusivity gave way after the Yom Kippur War, as U.S.-Arab relations gradually improved over the next two decades. After 1973, there was an incremental change in the United States' presence and role in the region — ties with both Israel and the Arab states expanded. At the same time the United States began a process of establishing links that presaged a substantial and multifaceted relationship that has grown to incorporate complex economic interrelationships including technical and economic assistance and military assistance and sales. The relationship with some of the Arab states, especially Saudi Arabia, gained new centrality in the Reagan administration, with its initial Persian Gulf-Southwest Asia focus and its concept of strategic consensus.

Israel's concern with the altering relationships, and the improved U.S. links with the Arab states, did not become a major public issue until early 1976, when proposed U.S. military sales to Saudi Arabia and Egypt became public knowledge. Israel opposed the sales, but the United States saw them as important for regional stability and peace, and for an improved relationship with the Arab states. United States plans to sell Egypt six C-130 military transport aircraft became a matter of major controversy. The United States saw this as an important factor to enhance Sadat's position, to encourage his moderation and movement away from the Soviet connection, and not affecting deleteriously the U.S.-Israel relationship. This foreshadowed the arms sales controversies of 1978 and 1981.

Examples of the discord and divergence in the policies and perceptions of the two states are numerous. On December 21, 1969, Israel's Cabinet issued a statement expressing its concern with the developing United States position as partly outlined in the Rogers plan of December 1969. It rejected the U.S. proposals because they prejudiced the peace process and, if implemented, would put Israel's security in very grave danger. In June 1981, Israel used aircraft supplied by the United States and crossed Jordanian and Saudi Arabian air space to destroy Iraq's Osirak nuclear reactor, embarrassing Washington and complicating its relations with the Arab states. The United States joined in the widespread condemnation of the raid and launched a review of whether Israel had violated the legal provisions of U.S.-Israel arms transfer agreements. During the review process, Washington suspended the shipment of F-16 aircraft to Israel. Also in the summer of 1981, Israeli aircraft struck PLO targets in populated West Beirut, killing several hundred civilians. This led to a further delay in the delivery of aircraft to Israel. In 1982 there was discord concerning the latter stages of the war in Lebanon, particularly the siege and occupation of Beirut, and the massacres in the Sabra and Shatilla camps.

The list goes on: the Pollard affair, in which an American was convicted of spying for Israel; the Iran-Contra affair; the Rami Dotan case, in which a senior Israeli general was implicated in a military procurement scandal involving the Israeli air force and General Electric officials; the accusations of technology transfer (including the Patriot missile to China issue); the failure of the peace effort by George Shultz in 1988 and later by James Baker in 1989 and 1990. In December 1987, the United States underlined its frustration and displeasure with Israel's use of force to quell the disturbances in the occupied territories by reissuing a travel advisory warning Americans to exercise care during visits to

Israel and those territories. In December 1981 Israel extended its law and jurisdiction to the Golan Heights (an act tantamount to annexation.) This action was not consonant with U.S. policy and, partly as a consequence, the United States suspended the 1981 memorandum of understanding on strategic cooperation. There was discord over the Lavi jet project, and it was eventually cancelled under strong United States pressure. The United States has expressed concern on a number of occasions over Israel's expulsions of Palestinians. In August 1988, Washington said it was "deeply concerned" over Israel's expanding use of expulsions to combat unrest in the occupied territories and "shocked" by Israel's decision to expel 25 more Palestinians. On January 5, 1988, the United States, for the first time since 1981, voted in favor of a United Nations resolution against Israel when it announced plans to begin expelling nine Palestinians.

On March 3, 1990, President Bush said that the United States opposed Soviet Jewish resettlement in the occupied territories, including East Jerusalem. This reiterated past policy that the United States opposed Israeli settlements in the occupied territory, and that East Jerusalem is part of the occupied territory that cannot be annexed unilaterally by Israel. Bush repeated this in a press conference in June. In the spring of 1990, many of Prime Minister Shamir's supporters believed that the Bush administration sought to undermine the government and to achieve the replacement of Shamir with a Peres-led Labor government. (Although a vote of no-confidence brought down the government, Peres failed in his efforts to forge a coalition and Shamir ultimately was successful in forming another government.)

The Bush administration was especially confrontational with respect to Israel. It made terse statements opposing "greater Israel," noting that the Israeli government should "call us if you're serious about peace." It linked humanitarian issues (loan guarantees for immigrant absorption) to political concessions, warned against "one thousand powerful lobbyists," and equated Jewish neighborhoods in East Jerusalem with West Bank settlements.

There were, are, and will be divergences that derive from differences of perspective in policy environments. The United States has broad concerns resulting from its global responsibilities. Israel's more restricted regional environment, the hostility and threat found within it, and its lesser responsibilities condition that state's perspective. Israel's horizon is more narrowly defined and is limited to the survival of the state and a concern for Jewish communities and individuals outside Israel, such as the Falashas of Ethiopia and the Jews of the Soviet Union.

Israel is a regional power with security as a central concern while the United States is a global power with global interests. The United States has a desire to have friendly relations with as many states as possible, including those Arab states in conflict with Israel, and is a major oil importing nation. This generates conflicts with Israel's concerns.

There has been a divergence on methods and techniques as well as discord on specific issues of various types, including the appropriate form of response to Arab terrorism, the value of great power efforts to resolve the conflict, the appropriateness and timing of face-to-face and direct Arab-Israeli negotiations, and the provision (types, quantities, and timing) of essential military supplies. During the Six Day War there was a clash over Israel's attack on the United States intelligence ship *Liberty*. In May 1968 there was disagreement over Israel's control of the islands of Tiran and Sanafir. The two states have disagreed on Israel's reprisals to Arab actions. After the Six Day War they disagreed over the limits placed by Israel on the refugees from the West Bank. They have had major disagreements concerning the occupied territories, their status, and Israel's role there, including the building of settlements. They have argued over Israel's desire for significant changes in the pre–Six Day War armistice lines as contrasted with the United States' perspective that there be "insubstantial alterations" or "minor modifications."

In many respects the issue of Jerusalem has highlighted the areas of discord. Jerusalem has been a matter of particular sensitivity because of its unique character and its significance to Judaism as well as to other major faiths, especially Islam. The United States supported the 1947 partition plan designation of Jerusalem as a separate entity and has stressed the international character of the city while refusing to recognize unilateral actions affecting its future. The United States refuses to move its embassy to Jerusalem, thus highlighting the differing perspectives. This has placed the two states in conflicting positions virtually continuously from 1947 to the present, especially since Israel's declarations of Jerusalem as the capital of the state and the reunification of the city during the 1967 war.

Personality clashes between senior U.S. and Israeli officials have also affected the tenor of the relationship. This was particularly evident in the relations between Jimmy Carter and Menachem Begin. During the Reagan administration mutual dislike and mistrust extended further — various United States officials were unhappy with Begin and Sharon; Israelis, in turn, were anxious about Secretary of Defense Caspar Weinberger's policies. The clash between Yitzhak Shamir, on the one hand, and George Bush and Jim Baker, on the other hand, was perhaps the most obvious.

There are limits on policy and decisions, but there are also self-imposed limits in the dealings of states, and these apply in the case of the U.S.-Israel relationship. There are limits to concessions that are possible despite extensive pressures. Israel will not "give in" on certain points, even under extensive pressure, and United States' efforts to induce changes in Israel's positions generally are cognizant of the limits beyond which it will achieve little, if any, policy modification. Core values and elements identified as matters of vital national interest are not susceptible to modification through influence. Yitzhak Shamir has commented: "On the fundamental life-and-death issues — such as security, Jerusalem, the 1967 borders, the danger of a Palestinian state — we have no choice but to stand by our position firmly, strongly and clearly — even against our great friend the United States."[1] Similar perspectives are regularly articulated by Rabin and his ministers.

Finally, it should be noted that Israeli decision makers respond to pressures exerted directly upon them with resentment and defiance. Pressure is an unacceptable interference in Israel's sovereign decision-making process and hence counterproductive. Israel will not rely on the wisdom of others on matters of vital national interest and overt efforts to exert such influence are doomed to failure. Because of this sensitivity, and because U.S. decision makers have understood it, the United States often has pursued the path of reassurance, indicating it would not use pressure to generate changes in Israeli policies, and providing tangible evidence of its support through military and economic aid and political and diplomatic action.

BETWEEN EUPHORIA AND DESPAIR

The special relationship has been characterized by periodic sharp oscillations. Each reversal of direction has tended to defy precise explanation and some have suggested that the nadir of the relationship has been reached and that the situation is now different from before. Thus, there have been traumas such as the pressure by the Eisenhower administration during the Suez Crisis in 1956–57, the Rogers Plan of December 1969, the reassessment of 1975, and the confrontation over loan guarantees in 1991–92.

In assessing the special relationship, however, it is important to distinguish between its two components: the basic underlying linkages and the facade. The first remains essentially constant, while the second is constantly shifting. It is the changes in the facade that are generally reported in the media and dominate public perceptions of the connection. But much of this facade is a function of the chemistry, or lack of it, between U.S. and Israeli leaders and of the general atmosphere. Behind the facade lie the fundamentals — basic shared values, the enduring place of Israel in the "mind of America," and strategic and political elements. At the core is the unique commitment on the part of the United States to the security of the Jewish state and the conviction that progress toward the peaceful resolution of the Arab-Israeli conflict is in the U.S. interest.

Periodically, journalists and other observers of the U.S.-Israel bilateral relationship offer sweeping assessments suggesting that the links have reached a new nadir and disaster is about to befall the connection between the two allies. Sometimes, reflecting ecstasy and euphoria, the opposite conclusion is reached. Periods of misunderstanding, friction, and confrontation, sometimes lengthy, sometimes brief, often alternate with periods of harmony and agreement.

During the spring of 1992, in the wake of the failure of Israel's efforts to secure loan guarantees and with charges being made that Israel had misused U.S. military technology, the relationship was marked by nasty charges and countercharges, tension, and stress. By the summer, after the Israeli Knesset elections, a euphoric mood dominated as Rabin became the Prime Minister and predictions of "sweetness and light" replaced an atmosphere of gloom. Former Foreign Minister Abba Eban has described this roller-coaster relationship: "One day they would pat you on the back and the next day kick you in the face."[2] It is a pendulum effect that fluctuates between the narrow confines imposed by their unique linkage.

What accounts for these swings of the pendulum? The asymmetries between the two states — their different sizes, places in the world order, and global outlooks — certainly play a part. Most significant, however, are the differences of expectations. For Israel, the relationship — especially the strategic connection — is vital. The United States is Israel's primary source of military equipment, as well as of political and diplomatic support. Their economic links are fundamental to Israel's economic health. For the United States, however, the relationship is much less significant. Measured in conventional terms, Israel is of limited military or economic importance to the United States. Israel's status as a democratic state commends it to the United States, but it is not a strategically vital state, nor is it likely to emerge as one.

What, therefore, will happen to the relationship if there is peace in the Middle East? Peace, defined as Israel's acceptance in the region, the elimination of war and terrorism as instruments of national or subnational policy, and the establishment of normal intercourse between the nations of the region, remains the primary object of Israeli policy. Thus, insofar as the United States helps to bring about this result, whatever short-term concerns Israel may harbor regarding U.S. policies, it will welcome the achievement. The process will not be tension-free: the two partners will continue to disagree on both the means to the end and the substance. But if peace comes, it should facilitate a closer relationship between the United States and Israel. The irritants endemic to the peace process itself will disappear, and the United States will no longer be forced to choose between Israel and the Arabs. Israel's need for military supply will be substantially reduced, and as the distorting aspects of the conflict on Israel's defense and overall budgets disappear, the country will be able to shift funds to productive areas. Cooperation between the United States and Israel in the strategic sphere will take on additional positive elements because Washington will no longer need to factor in Arab fears concerning Israel. In such an atmosphere, Israel would be able to join the coalition against Iraq, for example. The two states will also be able to expand on their natural connections that derive from their shared values.

The central conclusion is that until a comprehensive peace is achieved the bilateral special relationship between the United States and Israel is unlikely to be dramatically altered by the extensive shifts in the international system caused by the demise of the Soviet Union and the end of the Cold War or by the modifications in the Middle Eastern regional system associated with the Gulf War. Nor should it be. The bilateral relationship was never Cold War based, neither in its origins nor in its continuity. The United States-Soviet Union competition was, for some of the period after the Six Day War, a factor further expanding the strategic connection, but it was not its basis. Israel's focus on its survival and security, and consequently on the military balance and its need for arms acquisition, concentrated on the regional equilibrium, not on the Soviet factor.

The recommendations that flow from a reexamination of the special relationship are, in themselves, not extraordinary in content — essentially they argue for continuity, albeit with modifications, in virtually all sectors. The special relationship will, and should, be sustained for the various reasons already explored. History and the emotional-ideological linkages of these two states encompass the traditional connection. The political elements of the relationship are both widespread and legitimate within the U.S. political system. The strategic connection has helped to assure Israel's survival and security through the maintenance of its qualitative edge in relation to its potential adversaries. This, in turn, has been reinforced by economic assistance and support, which is also a measure of the close links between the two states.

Ultimately, in the bilateral special relationship, Israel will meet the tests of strategic utility and shared values as will the United States. The United States must sustain its special relationship and commitment to the survival and security of its democratic partner. In a world in which the United States dotes on emerging democracies and seeks to promote such democratic values worldwide, assuring the future of a state that is accountable to its people and that transfers power through orderly and peaceful change is a logical priority. The two states, however, will continue to disagree over many of the specifics, and the connection will be marked by both euphoria and despair as in the past. They will disagree on many aspects of the regional situation, the broader international environment, and the appropriate policies to respond to them while retaining common views on the need for peace and stability in the Middle East and for the survival and security of Israel.

Relations between the United States and Israel will continue to be viewed, discussed, analyzed, and determined with a passion reserved for few other connections. Israel and its special relationship with the United States remain controversial subjects of intense debate and discussion, although Israel's survival and security are the irreducible minimums even for the U.S. critics of the state and its links with the United States.

Relationships between friends and allies vary in quality and intensity over time. Even the most vaunted of the special relationships, that between the United States and Great Britain, recently has been called into question due to personal and policy differences between Britain's Prime Minister John Major and President Clinton. So, too, there have been similar factors affecting the warmth and robustness of the United States' special relationship with Israel. The world has changed and become more complex, and with that alteration the relevance and strength of the linkage between the United States and Israel has also been modified. Nevertheless, despite the personal suspicion and animus that will appear from time to time and policy differences resulting from divergent perspectives on important decisions that will develop, the two partners will survive these and other storms in their dealings and will continue to be connected in a special relationship that stresses the positive elements of their links in the areas of central importance to each. Israel's survival and security, and its quest for peace, will retain their centrality in U.S. policy, and Israel's commitment to the democratic (or "free") world, coupled with its espousal of free market economic systems, based on a long-standing historically and religiously based moral connection, will continue to assure the linkage to a U.S. government that places these values at the core of its system. U.S. military and economic assistance to ensure these objectives will continue (with modification to reflect the economic reality of the context in which policy decisions are made) to be an important element of the strategic connection and a meaningful measure of the relationship. The moral underpinnings of their connection and the confidence that they have established in each other are likely to continue to outweigh the crises that have and will develop in their relations. In the final analysis, the numerous links that bind them together will outweigh the often ephemeral issues and concerns that have worked to separate Washington and Jerusalem.

There are those who argue that it was only the glue of the Cold War that held the two together. The logical result of this perspective is that, without the anti-Soviet adhesive, the parties will inexorably be torn apart as Washington is drawn to other countries in the region that are economically more important because of their oil resources (for example, Saudi Arabia or Kuwait) and it will downplay the relationship with an Israel that has no significant quantities of that natural resource. The United States would discard the special place Israel has in U.S. perspective and policy and treat it like any other country. The evidence belies that conclusion.

Although the Soviet factor was an element in the strategic connection, especially during the Reagan administration, the U.S.-Israel linkage was not merely an alliance between partners in a strategic (anti-Soviet) venture, nor simply a relationship between those who view the world through a shared heritage summed up in the Judeo-Christian heritage of Western society. It is a complex amalgam of military, political, historical, ideological, moral, economic, and other elements that produces a new outcome best described as a special mixture not readily emulated by other powers.

The confluence of interests, and the willingness to pool resources and efforts to achieve and secure them, has varied over time — it was somewhat easier to speak of a strategic relationship when there was also a mutually-shared suspicion of Soviet policies and machinations in the Middle East. Nevertheless, there remains today a considerable overlap of core concerns (such as an Arab-Israeli peace, the security and well-being of Israel, and regional stability) on which the two countries can work together. At the same time, two different national entities will never be quite as selfless in supporting the other as the promoters of the relationship would have us believe. Just as the original special relationship between the United States and Great Britain had clashes (for example, in the Suez crisis of 1956 when the Eisenhower administration prevented a British-led tripartite effort to undermine Egypt's President Nasser and restore Britain to a favored position in regard to the Suez Canal), so will the one between the United States and Israel.

Policy differences and personal discord have, from time to time, coincided or led to one another. Ideological proclivities have also affected their connections; leaders have made a difference and personal chemistry is a factor. John Kennedy and David Ben Gurion reportedly connected well despite generational differences. Ronald Reagan and Menachem Begin often saw issues from a similar right of center perspective, and the domestic and foreign polices of each was guided by their ideological preferences. Truman was influenced by his meetings with Chaim Weizmann, the grand old man of Zionism and the first President of Israel. Others moved in divergent directions — none more clearly than George Bush and Yitzhak Shamir, who seemed to reinforce policy differences with clashing personalities.

Of course, the partnership is an unequal one — the United States is the world's only superpower (reluctance on the part of the Russian government to accept that fact notwithstanding) and Israel, despite its prowess in its region, remains a relatively puny power in the international community. The United States is larger, wealthier, considerably more powerful militarily, and is a political and diplomatic player of substantial importance with the capability to influence the direction of virtually all crucial international issues. However, they become more equal on issues of great importance to Israel and on matters affecting the neighborhood in which Israel is located. While there may be differences on specific tactics in the approach to regional Middle Eastern issues, they do see eye-to-eye on what, for Israel, are the most central concerns — resolving the Arab-Israeli conflict and ensuring the survival and security of Israel and Israelis.

This special relationship will continue to flourish in part because of a hospitable and supportive domestic environment. This nurturing environment, an outgrowth of the symbiotic interaction among the American Jewish community, public opinion, and Congress, has no precise parallel in other bilateral relationships. Episodes of discord in the formal relationship carried out by the executives of the two states have often been limited by the safety net provided Israel by a sympathetic Congress, buoyed by favorable public opinion, and influenced by an active Jewish community and pro-Israel lobby. Also, these same elements have helped to expand the bilateral relationship by sustaining numerous interactions at the unofficial level and by encouraging the executive branch to expand official links. Alterations in the policy environment and shifts in personnel have generated nuances of change in specific instances, and these will continue, but the overall reliability of Congress, public opinion, and the Israel lobby (with the Jewish community at its core) retains its basic importance.

Differences and discord, tensions, and even occasional clashes cannot obscure the fact that the covenant established between the United States and Israel defines a special relationship, in both form and substance, that is likely to be sustained into the twenty-first century.

Chronology of
U.S.-Israel Relations

1917   November 2   Balfour Declaration issued.

1922   September   Congress unanimously approves the Lodge-Fish resolution endorsing the Balfour Declaration.

1942   May   Biltmore Program promulgated.

1945   Anglo-American Committee of Inquiry established.

1947   November 29   Partition plan for Palestine adopted by UN General Assembly. United States supports the resolution.

       December 5   United States embargoes arms to the Middle East.

1948   March 19   United States proposes suspension of partition plan and calls for a temporary UN trusteeship over Palestine.

       May 14   State of Israel proclaimed as British mandate ends.

       May 15   Armies of Egypt, Iraq, Lebanon, Trans-Jordan, and Syria invade Israel and first Arab-Israeli

| | | War (Israel's War of Independence) officially begins. President Truman extends de facto recognition to Israel. |
| | May 17 | Soviet Union recognizes Israel. |

1949   January 19   U.S. Export-Import Bank announces a $35 million credit to Israel for agricultural projects and $65 million in credits for housing, communications, transportation, and manufacturing projects.

        January 25   First Knesset election.
        January 31   United States extends de jure recognition.
        February 16   Chaim Weizmann elected President.
        March 10   David Ben-Gurion becomes Israel's first Prime Minister.
        May 11   Israel becomes a member of the United Nations.
        December 13   Knesset decides to hold its sessions in Jerusalem.

1950   May 25   United States, Britain, and France issue Tripartite Declaration regulating arms to the Middle East.

1951   August 23   The United States and Israel sign a treaty of friendship, commerce, and navigation.

1952   July 23   Israel and the United States sign a mutual defense assistance agreement.

1953   May 11–29   U.S. Secretary of State John Foster Dulles visits Middle East.
        October 15   President Eisenhower appoints Eric Johnston to help establish Jordan River regional water development project.
        October 16   Syria complains to the UN regarding Israeli diversion of the Jordan River waters. U.S. economic assistance to Israel is stopped from October 20–28 until the latter agrees to halt work on the Jordan River project.

1954		American Zionist Committee for Public Affairs is established.
1955	August 26	Dulles proposes a plan for the settlement of the Arab-Israeli dispute.
	September 27	Egyptian-Czechoslovakian arms deal announced.
	October	Eric Johnston's plan for dividing the Jordan River water among Syria, Israel, Jordan, and Lebanon receives tentative approval from the states concerned.
	October 11	Arab League rejects Eric Johnston's Jordan River plan.
	October 18	Prime Minister Moshe Sharett applies to United States for permission to purchase arms.
1956	January 25	Ambassador Abba Eban requests Dulles' permission to acquire arms in the United States.
	February 8	Dulles says the United States will not sell arms to Israel.
	April 3	Dulles says the United States will not oppose arms shipments to Israel from other countries.
	May 9	Dulles tells the North Atlantic Treaty Organization that the United States will not sell arms to Israel directly in order to avoid U.S.-USSR confrontation in the Middle East.
	July 26	Egyptian President Gamal Abdul Nasser announces the nationalization of the Suez Canal Company.
	October 29	The Sinai Campaign begins. Israeli forces enter Sinai Peninsula to destroy Egyptian army and fedayeen bases and break naval blockade of Straits of Tiran.
	October 30	The United States calls an emergency session of the UN Security Council and introduces a resolution calling for an Israeli withdrawal. France and the United Kingdom veto the Soviet and U.S. resolutions for a cease-fire between Israel and Egypt.

November 5	General Assembly establishes United Nations Emergency Force. USSR threatens use of force if Britain, France, and Israel do not cease operations in Egypt.
November 7	General Assembly calls on Britain, France, and Israel to withdraw from Sinai Peninsula and Suez Canal zone. President Eisenhower demands Israeli compliance.
December 24	Beginning of Israeli forces withdrawal from Sinai.

1957	January–March	Israel evacuates the Sinai Peninsula.
	January 5	Eisenhower Doctrine announced.
	February	U.S. pressure on Israel to withdraw from Gaza and Sharm el-Sheikh. General Assembly considers sanctions against Israel.
	February 11	Dulles writes an aide memoire saying that the United States believes that the Gulf of Aqaba "comprehends international waters."
	March	Congress approves Eisenhower Doctrine.
	March 4	Ben Gurion orders the Israeli army to withdraw from the Gaza strip and the Gulf of Aqaba.
	March 10	Israel Defense Forces withdraws to armistice lines.
	April 21	United States resumes foreign assistance to Israel.
	June 3	Ben-Gurion announces acceptance of Eisenhower Doctrine.

| 1959 | | American Zionist Committee for Public Affairs renamed American Israel Public Affairs Committee. |

| 1960 | March 10 | Ben-Gurion meets with President Eisenhower at White House. |
| | December 20 | The State Department in Washington says that the United States is waiting for a reply to its request for information regarding the existence and purpose of the nuclear reactor plant in the |

		Rehovot region of Israel. Ambassador Avraham Harmon of Israel assures the U.S. government that Israel's nuclear reactor will not be used to make an atomic bomb.
	December 22	The State Department states that Israel's nuclear reactor no longer presents "a cause for special concern."
1961	May 23	Ben-Gurion visits Canada and the United States, meets with President Kennedy in New York.
1962	September 27	United States announces first direct sale of U.S. weapons (HAWK missiles) to Israel.
1964	January 15–17	Arab summit conference in Cairo discusses Jordan River diversion, establishment of a joint military command, and establishment of Palestine Liberation Organization.
	May 31–June 2	Prime Minister Levi Eshkol visits President Johnson; first official visit of an Israeli Prime Minister.
	June	Israel's National Water Carrier begins operations.
	September 5	An Arab summit conference opens in Cairo. It adopts a plan to divert the headwaters of the Jordan River.
1966	May 18	Eshkol declares that Israel will not be the first to introduce nuclear weapons into the Middle East.
	May 19	United States confirms sale of A-4 Skyhawk jet fighter aircraft to Israel.
	November 14	Israel raids Samu village following incursions from Jordan.
	November 25	The Security Council condemns Israel for the attack on Samu.
1967	May 15	The United Arab Republic puts its forces on a state of alert and begins extensive redeployment of military units.

May 18	The United Arab Republic asks the United Nations to remove United Nations Emergency Force from the Egypt-Israel armistice line and the United Nations complies.	
May 22	United Arab Republic President Gamal Abdul Nasser announces an Egyptian blockade of the Gulf of Aqaba.	
May 23	President Lyndon Johnson reiterates that the United States is "firmly committed to the support of the political independence and territorial integrity of all the nations in the area."	
May 26	Foreign Minister Eban meets Johnson.	
June 5	Third Arab-Israeli (Six Day) War begins.	
June 10	The USSR breaks diplomatic relations with Israel. Other Eastern bloc states, except Romania, follow.	
June 12	Israel announces it will not withdraw to 1949 armistice lines before peace is achieved by direct negotiations.	
June 19	Johnson outlines principles for peace in the Middle East, establishing a framework for subsequent U.S. policy.	
June 28	Israel proclaims unification of Jerusalem within new municipal boundaries.	
September 1	Arab summit conference in Khartoum proclaims policy of no peace, no recognition, and no negotiations with Israel.	
November 22	UN Security Council adopts Resolution 242; Gunnar Jarring appointed special representative of the Secretary General.	
December	The United States begins shipping A-4 Skyhawk jet aircraft to Israel.	

1968	February 7	Eshkol ends two days of talks with President Johnson in Texas.
	March 21	Israel Defense Forces raids village of Karameh in Jordan to prevent massing of terrorists.
	July 18	An amendment to the Foreign Assistance Act states that it is the sense of the Congress that

	the United States should sell jet aircraft to Israel.
October 9	Johnson announces negotiations for the sale of 50 F-4 Phantom jet aircraft to Israel.
December	President-elect Richard Nixon's special envoy Governor Scranton pledges a more "even-handed" U.S. policy.
December 27	United States announces sale of 50 Phantom F-4 jets to Israel.

1969	April	War of Attrition begins along the Suez Canal.
	March 14	Foreign Minister Eban meets President Nixon. Israel denounces four-power attempts to reach a settlement.
	December 9	Secretary of State William Rogers announces peace plan based on Israeli withdrawal in exchange for binding peace treaty with Arabs.
	December 22	Israel's cabinet issues a statement expressing its concern with the developing United States policy as outlined in the Rogers Plan and rejects the proposals.

1970	March 23	Rogers states that the Israeli request for 25 F-4 Phantoms and 100 Skyhawks will be held in abeyance because the United States does not believe Israel needs the weapons at that time.
	April	Israel notes that Soviet pilots are flying operational missions for Egyptian air force.
	June 25	Rogers discloses U.S. initiative to end war of attrition along Suez Canal for 90 days and resume stalled Jarring mission.
	July 23	Egypt accepts U.S. initiative.
	August 4	Israel accepts U.S. initiative and is assured of continued military and economic aid.
	August 7	Cease-fire goes into effect on Suez Canal. Egypt violates cease-fire. Israel protests to United States.
	September	Jordan crisis and civil war. Heavy fighting between Jordanian army and Palestinians. Syria moves troops into Jordan. United States moves Sixth Fleet to Eastern Mediterranean.

	September 18	Prime Minister Golda Meir meets Nixon. Israel refuses to return to Jarring talks until Egyptian missiles are withdrawn.
1971	January 5	Jarring talks resume.
	February 9	Israel and Egypt accept in principle the idea of interim agreement for reopening of Suez Canal.
	May 1	Rogers visits Middle East for talks on interim agreement.
	October 6	Israel and Egypt reject Rogers proposals presented on October 4 in UN General Assembly.
	December 2	Prime Minister Meir meets President Nixon in Washington.
1973	March 1	Meir meets Nixon in Washington.
	October 6	The Fifth Arab-Israeli (Yom Kippur) War begins. Egyptian forces cross Suez Canal, Syrian forces attack Israel on Golan Heights.
	October 15	United States starts air lift to Israel.
	October 19	Nixon asks Congress to appropriate $2.2 billion for emergency aid to Israel, including direct military grants.
	October 20	Secretary of State Henry Kissinger arrives in Moscow for talks.
	October 22	UN Security Council adopts Resolution 338.
	October 25	United States alerts forces to DEFCON 3.
	October 31	Meir arrives in Washington for talks with Nixon and Kissinger.
	November	Agranat Commission established.
	December 21	Geneva Peace Conference on Middle East is held.
1974	January	Shuttle diplomacy by Kissinger to bring about Israeli-Egyptian separation of forces agreement.
	January 18	Israel-Egypt separation of forces agreement is signed at kilometer 101 on the Cairo-Suez road.

February 28	United States and Egypt resume full diplomatic relations.
May 31	Israeli-Syrian disengagement agreement brokered by Kissinger is signed.
June 12	Nixon visits the Middle East.
June 16	United States and Syria resume diplomatic relations.
June 16–17	Nixon visits Israel.
August 10	President Gerald Ford assures Israel the United States will honor its commitments.
September 10–13	Prime Minister Yitzhak Rabin pays an official visit to Washington.
October 26–30	Arab summit conference in Rabat determines that the Palestine Liberation Organization is the sole legitimate representative of the Palestinian Arabs.
November 1	Israel announces there will be no talks with the Palestine Liberation Organization.

1975	January 16	Foreign Minister Yigal Allon holds talks in Washington with Ford and Kissinger.
	March 8	Kissinger starts his shuttles between Jerusalem and Cairo to obtain the interim agreement.
	March 22	Kissinger's talks are suspended.
	March 23	Ford orders "reassessment" of U.S. Middle East policy after suspension of the Kissinger shuttle effort.
	May	Seventy-six senators write to President Ford reaffirming their support for Israel in light of recent developments that suggest that the administration is acting in a manner critical of Israel.
	June 10–11	Rabin meets with Ford in Washington.
	September 1	Israel-Egypt disengagement agreement (Sinai II) is initialed in Jerusalem and Alexandria. The United States pledges not to recognize or negotiate with the Palestine Liberation Organization so long as it does not recognize Israel's right to exist, does not accept UN Security Council resolutions 242 and 338, and continues to engage in terrorism.

September 4	Sinai II Agreement is signed in Geneva.
September 17–20	Defense Minister Peres visits Washington for talks on arms deliveries.
September 22	Military protocol for implementation of the Sinai II agreement is signed in Geneva by Egypt, initialed by Israel.
October 10	Israel signs the military protocol after Congress approves U.S. presence in Sinai. Abu Rudeis oil fields returned to Egypt.
November 10	The UN General Assembly adopts a resolution equating Zionism with racism.
November 11	Congress unanimously calls for a reassessment of the U.S. relationship with the UN after it adopts the "Zionism is racism" resolution.

1976	January 26–29	Prime Minister Rabin pays an official visit to the United States and addresses a joint session of Congress.
	February 22	Israel Defense Forces completes withdrawal under the Sinai II agreement.
	March 22	The United States vetoes an anti-Israel draft resolution at the conclusion of a Security Council discussion on the situation in the West Bank.
	August 5	Israel and the United States initial an agreement for the supply to Israel of two nuclear reactors.

1977	February 17	Secretary of State Vance holds talks in Jerusalem.
	March 7–9	Prime Minister Rabin visits Washington for talks with President Carter.
	March 16	Carter endorses a Palestinian "homeland" in address at Clinton, Massachusetts.
	June 22	Prime Minister Menachem Begin accepts an invitation by Carter to visit Washington on July 18–20.
	June 27	State Department spokesman reiterates Carter administration Middle East policy, saying that Israel should negotiate withdrawal from the West Bank and Gaza, among other items.

June 28	Israel rejects implications of U.S. statement, saying Israel is ready to negotiate every issue.
July 6	United States rejects Israeli request to sell 24 Kfir fighter-bombers to Ecuador.
July 19–21	Begin and Carter meet in Washington and reach agreement on the need for Israel to negotiate with the Arab states in the framework of a Geneva conference.
July 31	Secretary of State Cyrus Vance leaves on a 12-day visit to the Middle East, bearing U.S. proposals for a Geneva peace conference.
August 8	Carter says that if Palestine Liberation Organization accepts UNSC Resolution 242 in its entirety, the United States will start discussions with this organization.
August 9	Israel rejects any idea of Palestine Liberation Organization participation in the peace negotiations even if it accepts Resolution 242.
August 10	Vance holds talks in Jerusalem on the proposed Foreign Ministers conference in September.
August 23	Carter again criticizes Israel on the settlement issue but says the United States will not exert any military or other pressure to stop the settlements.
September 23	In a meeting with Foreign Minister Moshe Dayan, Carter calls for a single unified Arab delegation at the opening of the Geneva conference that would contain Palestinians who are not known leaders of the Palestine Liberation Organization.
September 26	In a meeting with Vance, Dayan rejects participation of any Palestine Liberation Organization member in the Arab delegation.
October 1	United States and the Soviet Union issue a joint communique on the Middle East.
October 5	Carter and Dayan agree on a "working paper" detailing procedures for a Geneva conference.
October 18	Zbigniew Brzezinski says United States has the right to exert leverage on Middle East parties to encourage them to move toward settlement.

October 19	United States sends an amended version of the Israel-U.S. working paper on Geneva conference to Cairo.
November 9	Sadat announces his readiness to come to Jerusalem to address the Knesset in the search for peace.
November 15	Begin sends written invitation to Sadat to come to Jerusalem. Sadat says his trip is a holy mission.
November 19	Sadat arrives in Israel and receives a state welcoming ceremony at Ben-Gurion airport. Meets with Begin in Jerusalem.
November 20	Sadat addresses the Knesset, calling for Israeli withdrawal and the establishment of a Palestinian state.
December 16–17	Begin and Carter meet in Washington. Sadat invites Begin for talks with him in Egypt.
December 25	Begin and Sadat meet in Ismailiya, agree to constitute Israel-Egypt political and military committees.
December 28	Carter praises Begin peace plan, but prefers a Palestinian homeland or entity linked to Jordan.
1978 January 4	Carter and Sadat meet in Aswan, issue the "Aswan proclamation" calling for the recognition of the legitimate rights of the Palestinian people and their participation in the determination of their future.
January 26	U.S. Assistant Secretary of State Alfred Atherton arrives in Israel to start shuttle diplomacy for the attainment of an Israel-Egypt declaration of principles prior to resumption of peace talks.
February 2	Carter administration proposes to Congress a "package deal" for the sale of jet aircraft to Israel, Egypt, and Saudi Arabia.
February 15	U.S. threatens to withdraw Israel request for jet aircraft if Congress blocks sale to Saudi Arabia and Egypt.

March 11	Arab terrorists hijack buses on the Haifa-Tel Aviv road, leaving 37 civilians dead and scores injured.
March 14	Israel Defense Forces cross the Lebanese border and seize a 7-mile strip along the border. Begin says Israel Defense Forces will remain in Lebanon until an agreement is reached ensuring the area will no longer serve as terrorist base.
March 19	Israel Defense Forces take over entire Southern Lebanon to the Litani River as United States seeks UN Security Council resolution that will send an international force to replace the Israel Defense Forces. Security Council adopts Resolution 425, calling for immediate withdrawal of Israeli troops from Lebanon and the stationing of a UN force there.
March 21–22	Begin and Carter hold two days of talks in White House. United States and Israel are in disagreement over a number of issues. UN forces arrive in Southern Lebanon.
March 24	Carter details the area of Israel-U.S. disagreement, calls on Israel to make concessions. Begin returns to Israel.
April 11	Israel Defense Forces start withdrawal from Lebanon.
May 16	Senate approves the sale of warplanes to Israel, Egypt, and Saudi Arabia. Israel expresses its regret.
June 13	Israel Defense Forces complete withdrawal from Lebanon.
June 30–July 3	Vice President Walter Mondale visits Israel.
August 5–7	Secretary Vance visits Israel and Egypt, and following his talks Sadat and Begin agree to take part in the Camp David summit in September.
August 17	President Carter announces that the United States will be a full and equal partner in the Camp David talks.
September 5–17	Camp David summit conference. It ends in the signing, at the White House, of two

	documents: "A Framework for Peace in the Middle East" and "Framework for the Conclusion of a Peace Treaty Between Egypt and Israel."
September 27	The Knesset approves the Camp David Accords.
October 12	Opening of the talks at Blair House on the Israel-Egypt peace treaty.
October 27	Sadat and Begin win the Nobel Peace prize.

1979	February 25	To break the Egypt-Israel deadlock over the peace treaty, Carter invites Begin and Egyptian Prime Minister Mustafa Khalil to meet with him in Washington.
	February 27	Israel rejects the Carter invitation. Begin expresses readiness to meet with Carter alone.
	February 28	Carter invites Begin for talks in Washington.
	March 1–4	Begin-Carter talks in the White House.
	March 7	President Carter announces he will visit Israel and Egypt in a last-minute effort to conclude the treaty.
	March 10–13	Carter visits Israel and wins additional concessions from Israel.
	March 14	Sadat accepts the last-minute changes brought from Jerusalem by Carter, thus paving the way for the signing of the peace treaty.
	March 26	The Egypt-Israel Peace Treaty is signed at the White House.
	April 23	State Department deplores an Israeli government decision to establish two settlements in Samaria.
	May 25	Israel begins withdrawal from the Sinai Peninsula; Egypt and Israel begin discussion of autonomy issues.
	July 2–3	Newly appointed U.S. special envoy for the autonomy talks, Robert Strauss, meets with Begin in Jerusalem and Sadat in Alexandria.
	November 7	Ambassador Sol Linowitz succeeds Strauss as the U.S. special envoy for the autonomy talks.

1980	February 26	Egypt and Israel exchange ambassadors.
	March 1	The UN Security Council adopts a resolution calling on Israel to dismantle existing settlements and discontinue establishing new settlements. United States votes in favor. Later Carter disavowed the vote saying it was the result of communications failure.
	April 30	United States vetoes a Security Council draft resolution calling for the creation of a Palestinian state.
	May 8	Security Council votes for a resolution calling on Israel to rescind the deportation of the mayors of Hebron and Halhoul. The United States abstains.
	May 20	Security Council deplores Israel's failure to return the deported mayors. United States abstains.
	June 30	Security Council adopts a resolution deploring moves by Israel to make the whole of Jerusalem the capital of Israel. United States abstains.
	July 30	The Knesset votes by 69 to 15 with 3 abstentions to approve Basic Law: Jerusalem, reaffirming united Jerusalem as Israel's capital.
	August 20	Security Council votes to condemn Israel for the passage of the Jerusalem law and urges all nations not to recognize it. United States abstains.
	October 17	Israel and the United States sign an agreement guaranteeing the supply of oil to Israel in times of specified emergencies.
1981	February 24	Foreign Minister Shamir meets President Ronald Reagan at the White House.
	April 22	Israel condemns the U.S. decision to supply sophisticated weapons to Saudi Arabia.
	June 6	Israel destroys Osirak nuclear reactor near Baghdad.
	June 10	United States suspends arms deliveries to Israel in the wake of the Baghdad raid.

June 20	Security Council condemns Israel for the raid on the Iraqi nuclear reactor.
July 13	Begin meets with Ambassador Phillip Habib and Counsellor Robert McFarlane in an effort to defuse the tension between Israel and the United States and to ease the tension along Israel's northern border.
July 21	Israel's government authorizes Habib to negotiate a cease fire with the President of Lebanon.
July 24	Israel accepts a cease fire proposal brought by Habib.
July 28	The Knesset approves the agreement for the creation of a multinational force in Sinai.
September 6–16	Begin, accompanied by Ministers Yitzhak Shamir, Ariel Sharon, and Yosef Burg, visits Washington for talks with Reagan on U.S. arms sale to Saudi Arabia and a U.S.-Israel strategic cooperation agreement.
October 29	Israel condemns a Senate vote to approve sale of Airborne Warning and Control Systems to Saudi Arabia.
November 30	Defense Minister Ariel Sharon and Secretary of Defense Caspar Weinberger sign, in Washington, a Memorandum of Understanding on Strategic Cooperation between the United States and Israel.
December 14	The Knesset approves the Golan Heights Law extending Israel's law and jurisdiction there.
December 17	The United States joins in a unanimous UN Security Council resolution condemning the Israeli move, declaring the annexation "null and void."
December 18	The United States suspends implementation of the strategic cooperation agreement. The Security Council calls on Israel to rescind the Golan Heights Law.
December 20	Begin informs Ambassador to Israel Samuel Lewis that Israel views the suspension of the strategic cooperation agreement as tantamount

to its annulment. Begin also castigates Lewis
for thinking of Israel as a "banana republic".

1982	January 15	Secretary of State Alexander Haig visits Israel.
	January 20	Moshe Arens is appointed as Israel's Ambassador to Washington.
	February 15	The Knesset expresses its regrets over U.S. sale of F-16 and HAWK missiles to Jordan.
	April 25	Israel completes its withdrawal from the Sinai Peninsula, except for disputed territory at Taba, and multinational forces assume peacekeeping responsibilities.
	May 25	Sharon holds talks in Washington with Haig and Weinberger.
	June 6	Israel launches Operation Peace for Galilee to destroy Palestine Liberation Organization bases in Lebanon as Israel Defense Forces cross the Lebanese border and advance into Lebanon.
	June 9	United States vetoes a Security Council draft resolution condemning the Israeli operation.
	June 10	Reagan demands an immediate cease fire. Israel accepts his call.
	June 21	Begin and Reagan meet in the White House.
	June 26	UN General Assembly adopts a resolution calling for an end to hostilities and immediate unconditional withdrawal of Israel from Lebanon (127 to 2).
	July 4	Israel Defense Forces begin to besiege West Beirut. Israel allows Ambassador Habib additional time to continue his efforts to bring about the Palestine Liberation Organization withdrawal.
	July 19	Reagan orders the hold up of cluster bombs for Israel.
	August 2	In a meeting with Shamir, Reagan demands that Israel cease all hostilities in Beirut. Israel agrees to allow Ambassador Habib additional time for his diplomatic efforts.
	August 4	Israel Defense Forces intensify the siege of West Beirut. Reagan demands Begin bring an

	immediate halt to the shelling of Beirut and threatens to review U.S.-Israel relations.
August 12	Israeli jets carry out massive air raids on Beirut. Reagan phones Begin demanding an end to the bombing. Begin agrees.
September 1	Reagan announces a "fresh start" initiative for peace in the Middle East.
September 5	Begin informs Reagan that Israel will not negotiate on the basis of the Reagan Plan and complains about the absence of prior consultations with Israel.
September 15	Israel Defense Forces seize West Beirut and surround the Palestinian refugee camps of Sabra and Shatilla without entering them.
September 16–18	Phalange forces carry out massacres in the Sabra and Shatilla camps killing hundreds of civilians. Israel is accused of being indirectly responsible for the crime.
September 28	Israel government resolves to establish a commission of inquiry and Justice Kahan names himself its chairman.
December 28	Israel-Lebanon negotiations open in Khalde, with U.S. participation. Lebanon demands full Israeli withdrawal and the return to the 1949 Armistice Lines. Israel views this agreement as void because of Lebanon's declaration of war in 1967.

1983

January 2–15	President Yitzhak Navon pays an official visit to the United States.
January 23	Israel rejects U.S. protests over clashes between the Israel Defense Forces and U.S. Marines patrolling in Beirut.
February 8	The Kahan commission issues its final report. It finds Israel indirectly responsible for not anticipating the consequences of the Phalange entry into the camps and recommends the removal of Sharon and a number of senior officers from their posts.
February 13	Sharon resigns from his office but remains in the Cabinet as Minister without Portfolio.

	Moshe Arens becomes Defense Minister.
March 13	Shamir visits Washington and holds talks with Reagan and Secretary of State George Shultz in an effort to coordinate Israeli and U.S. positions on Lebanon.
April 10	The Cabinet rejects U.S. claims that settlement in the territories impedes the peace process.
April 13	Habib holds talks in Jerusalem on the proposed agreement with Lebanon.
April 17	Pentagon announces approval of Israeli use of U.S. components and technology to build the Lavi fighter aircraft.
May 17	The Israel-Lebanon agreement is signed in Khalde and Kiryat Shmona.
July 6	Secretary of State Shultz makes a brief visit to Israel.
July 26–28	Shamir and Arens hold talks in Washington with Reagan and senior officials on the Israeli redeployment plan.
August 3	U.S. Special Envoy Robert McFarlane holds talks in Israel. The United States vetoes an anti-Israeli draft resolution in the Security Council.
October 23	241 U.S. Marines, part of the multinational force, are killed in a truck bomb attack in Lebanon.
October 29	Reagan signs National Security Decision Directive 111 providing guidelines for U.S.-Israel strategic cooperation.
November 14–24	President Chaim Herzog pays an official visit to the United States.
November 28	Prime Minister Shamir and Arens hold talks in the White House and reach an agreement on joint Israel-U.S. strategic, political, military, and economic cooperation.
November 29	Shamir and Reagan establish a Joint Political-Military Group to meet regularly to discuss military issues. They also agree to negotiate the establishment of a Free Trade Area.

1984	January 8	Chairman of the U.S. Joint Chiefs of Staff General John Vessey visits Israel.
	February 21	U.S. peacekeeping force departs Lebanon.
	March 5	Lebanon abrogates the May 17, 1983, Israel-Lebanon agreement.
	May 30	Arens pays an official visit to Washington.
	June 20	Israel and the United States hold joint military exercises.
	October 15	Defense Secretary Caspar Weinberger arrives in Israel on a two day visit.
	December 11	U.S. and Israeli naval units hold joint maneuvers in the eastern Mediterranean.
1985	January 30	Defense Minister Yitzhak Rabin meets with Reagan in the White House. The United States announces that Israel will receive $1.8 billion in military aid for the next fiscal year.
	March 7	Finance Minister Yitzhak Modai signs in Washington the U.S.-Israel Free Trade Zone agreement.
	April 5	The United States invites Israel to participate in research for the Strategic Defense Initiative (also known as Star Wars).
	May 1	The United States authorizes $1.5 billion emergency aid to Israel.
	August 1	Congress approves a $3 billion aid package to Israel ($1.2 billion economic and $1.8 billion military).
	August 24	The U.S.-Israel Free Trade Area Agreement is ratified.
	October 1	Israeli jets bomb Palestine Liberation Organization headquarters in Tunisia.
	October 3	The United States abstains during a Security Council vote condemning Israel for the attack.
	November 21	Jonathan Pollard is arrested in Washington and is charged with spying for Israel.
1986	July 27–30	Vice President George Bush visits Israel.
1987	February 9	The first F-16 jet fighters arrive in Israel.

March 27	Reagan and Israel's Minister of Communications sign a Voice of America agreement permitting construction of a relay transmitter in Israel.
August 30	Israel decides to halt the production of the Lavi.
October 16	Shultz visits Israel for talks on a formula to renew the peace process.
November 9–16	Herzog pays an official visit to the United States.
December 8–10	Palestinian uprising (intifada) erupts in the Gaza Strip and quickly spreads to the West Bank.
December 14	Rabin and Secretary of Defense Frank Carlucci sign in Washington a Memorandum of Understanding valid for ten years that codifies the rules for military commerce between the two countries. Israel is formally designated "a major non-NATO ally."

1988

January 5	The United States, for the first time since 1981, votes in favor of a United Nations resolution against Israel when it announces plans to begin expelling nine Palestinians.
January 30	Prime Minister Shamir expresses reservations over Shultz's plan, which includes an interim arrangement for the inhabitants of the territories, an international opening session, and bilateral talks on permanent settlement.
February 25	Shultz arrives in Israel to promote his peace initiative.
March 4	Secretary Shultz formally presents his proposals for the resumption of the peace process.
March 14–16	Shamir meets in Washington with Reagan, Shultz, and other leading members of the administration as well as Congressional leaders.
April 3	Shultz arrives in Israel for another round of talks on his peace plan.

April 21	Israel and the United States sign a Memorandum of Understanding dealing with military, political, economic, and scientific cooperation.
May 17	Foreign Minister Peres meets in Washington with Reagan and senior administration officials.
June 5	Shultz visits Israel again to promote his peace initiative.
June 27–28	Rabin holds talks in Washington with Reagan and Carlucci. At the conclusion of the visit the White House issues a statement announcing joint Israel-U.S. development of the Arrow anti-missile missile and re-affirming the U.S. commitment to Israel's security.
December 13	Arafat addresses United Nations in Geneva; says Palestine National Council accepts UNSC Resolutions 242 and 338 and rejects terrorism.
December 14	Arafat, at press conference, recognizes Israel's right to exist, accepts UNSC Resolutions 242 and 338, and renounces terrorism. The United States decides to enter into a dialogue with the Palestine Liberation Organization. Israel expresses its dismay. Reagan and Shultz send messages of explanation to Israel.

1989	January 17	The Knesset unanimously adopts a resolution calling on Bush to pardon Jonathan Pollard.
	April 5–6	Shamir leaves for an unofficial visit to Washington.
	May 14	The Israeli cabinet formally approves a four-point plan for Palestinian elections in the West Bank and Gaza Strip. The United States accepts it as a basis for the peace process.
	June	Ninety-five senators write to Secretary of State James Baker "to express our support for the peace initiative recently launched by the Government of Israel."
	October 6	Baker proposes five-point plan to Israel.
	October 23	Israel requests modifications in Baker's five-point plan.

1990	February 22	Arens meets Baker in Washington. Shamir, in a telephone conversation with Bush, promises not to settle Soviet Jewish immigrants in the territories.
	March 3	Bush says that the United States opposes Soviet Jewish settlement in the occupied territories, including East Jerusalem.
	March 24	Senate adopts a resolution recognizing Jerusalem as Israel's capital.
	April 24	House of Representatives adopts a resolution recognizing Jerusalem as the capital of Israel.
	May 31	The United States vetoes a draft resolution in the Security Council to send an observer to the territories.
	June 20	United States suspends its dialogue with the Palestine Liberation Organization for its failure to condemn a May 30 terrorist attack on Israel.
	July 12	Chairman of the Joint Chiefs of Staff, General Powell, visits Israel.
	July 19	Arens visits Washington and holds talks with Defense Secretary Dick Chaney.
	August 2	Iraq invades Kuwait.
	October 2	Israel gets $400 million loan guarantee. Israel tells the United States that it will not settle new immigrants in the territories.
	October 8	In an incident on the Temple Mount in Jerusalem, 21 Arabs are killed and scores injured by the Israeli police.
	December 11	Following a meeting with Bush in the White House, Shamir says that he was promised there would be no deals at Israel's expense.
1991	January	In an effort to widen the Gulf War, Iraq launches Scud missiles against Israel. Israel decides not to retaliate in response to U.S. request.
	January 26	At the conclusion of a meeting in Washington between Baker and the Soviet foreign minister, they call for joint U.S.-Soviet efforts to promote Arab-Israel peace and regional stability.

February 28	Israel congratulates Bush as the Gulf War comes to an end. Israel demands the elimination of Iraqi weapons of mass destruction.
March	Baker makes first of a series of visits to the Middle East partly to pursue an Arab-Israeli peace settlement.
September 5	The United States announces it will delay action on Israel's request for $10 billion in loan guarantees to aid in the resettlement of Soviet Jewish immigrants.
September 12	George Bush challenged the pro-Israel lobby by stating that $10 billion in loan guarantees to Israel would contribute to the further extension of Israeli settlements in the occupied territories, a policy he opposed as an obstacle to peace.
October 18	Baker visits Israel. Bush and President Mikhail Gorbachev invite the parties to the Madrid Peace Conference. Israel and the Soviet Union restore diplomatic relations. The United States delivers a letter of assurances to the Palestinians.
October 30–31	Middle East peace conference is held in Madrid, Spain.
December 10	Beginning of Washington rounds of bilateral Arab-Israeli negotiations.
December 16	UN General Assembly repeals Resolution 3379 that had equated Zionism with racism.
1992 August 10–11	Prime Minister Rabin visits President Bush at his summer home in Kennebunkport, Maine. Bush announces he will ask Congress to approve the $10 billion in loan guarantees.
December	Israel deports more than 400 Islamic fundamentalists from the occupied territories into southern Lebanon.
1993	Secret negotiations between Israel and Palestine Liberation Organization take place in Oslo, Norway.

	July	Israel launches Operation Accountability into Lebanon.
	September 13	Israel-Palestine Liberation Organization Declaration of Principles signed on the White House lawn in Washington, D.C.
	October	Negotiations begin between Israel and Palestine Liberation Organization to implement Declaration of Principles.
1994	January	President Bill Clinton meets with President Hafez al-Assad in Geneva to further the Arab-Israeli negotiations.
	February	Massacre at the Ibrahim Mosque in Hebron.
	May 4	Rabin and Arafat sign agreement regarding the Gaza Strip and Jericho in Cairo.
	July 25	King Hussein of Jordan and Yitzhak Rabin meet at the summit in Washington and issue the Washington Declaration.

Notes

CHAPTER 1

1. Embassy of Israel, Washington, D.C., *For Your Information*, "Presentation of the New Government: Address before Knesset by Prime Minister Designate Yitzhak Rabin, 13 July 1992," n.p.

2. "B'nai B'rith: The President's Remarks at the 125th Anniversary Meeting, September 10, 1968," *Weekly Compilation of Presidential Documents*, September 16, 1968, p. 1343.

3. Jimmy Carter, *Keeping Faith: Memoirs of a President* (New York: Bantam Books, 1982), p. 274.

4. Vice President Walter Mondale at the American Jewish Committee, New York, May 18, 1978. Emphasis in original.

5. "Democracy in America," remarks by Governor Bill Clinton, University of Wisconsin, Milwaukee, October 1, 1992, p. 1.

6. Ibid., pp. 3–4.

7. Assistant Secretary of State Edward Djerejian, June 24, 1992. Reaffirming this conception, President Bill Clinton, in a joint press conference on March 16, 1994, with Prime Minister Yitzhak Rabin, said, "Since the beginning of this administration, the Prime Minister and I have worked to promote the common interest and values our nations share. Today we are working closely together on such issues. . . . Our efforts have one common purpose: maintaining the principles we both share while doing all we can to promote peace."

CHAPTER 2

1. The War of Independence (1948–49), the Suez War (1956–57), the Six Day War (June 1967), the War of Attrition (1969–70), the Yom Kippur War (1973), and the War in Lebanon (1982).

2.   In 1955 then Israel Defense Forces Chief-of-Staff, Moshe Dayan, wrote in *Foreign Affairs*: "There is no other state . . . whose very right to existence is so persistently challenged by all its contiguous neighbors." A decade later then Chief-of-Staff Yitzhak Rabin noted the Arab aim is the destruction of the State of Israel. In *David's Sling* (1970), Shimon Peres, then a government minister and later prime minister, foreign minister, and Labor Party leader, described the Arab purpose as "the destruction of Israel and the annihilation or banishment of her inhabitants." In 1976, Foreign Minister Yigal Allon wrote: "The Arab states seek to isolate, strangle and erase Israel from the world's map . . . a military defeat of Israel would mean the physical extinction of a large part of its population and the political elimination of the Jewish state." Reflecting this view, in the late 1960s Yehoshafat Harkabi, a former general in the Israel Defense Forces and then a professor at Hebrew University, coined the term "politicide" (the liquidation of a state) to describe the Arab goal of eliminating Israel.

3.   In November 1975 the United Nations General Assembly adopted a resolution in which it determined "that Zionism is a form of racism and social discrimination." In December 1991 the General Assembly adopted a U.S.-sponsored resolution revoking the earlier decision. The Arab states opposed the repeal.

4.   The term "fundamentalism" is widely used by U.S. and other commentators to refer to extremism and the militant groups that advocate it. It is imprecise and somewhat misleading, but provides a convenient shorthand to refer to those who pervert Islam for political purposes and pose a threat, often violent in nature, to legitimate regimes. It is in that sense that it is employed here.

5.   This point is reinforced by the DOP process for, although the initial negotiations took place in Norway, the signature on September 13, 1993, and the post-signing process again focused on Washington and the U.S. role. Similarly, Israel and Jordan issued their joint declaration in Washington in July 1994.

CHAPTER 3

1.   Jimmy Carter, *Keeping Faith: Memoirs of a President* (New York: Bantam Books, 1982), pp. 274–75.

2.   "U.S., Israel Agree on Strategic Cooperation," *Department of State Bulletin*, January 1982, p. 45.

3.   "Remarks of the President and Prime Minister Yitzhak Shamir of Israel Upon Departure," White House Press Release, November 29, 1983, p. 1.

4.   The project was cancelled in 1993.

5.   White House Statement, April 21, 1988, White House Press Release, reprinted in *Department of State Bulletin*, June 1988, p. 39.

6.   *New York Times*, May 13, 1977.

7.   Quoted in *The Jerusalem Post*, January 6, 1981.

8.   U.S. Senate, Committee on Foreign Relations, *Report, National Commitment*, 91st Cong., 1st Sess., April 16, 1969, pp. 26–27.

9.   The United States wrote to Israel as follows: "The United States will continue to adhere to its present policy with respect to the Palestine Liberation Organization, whereby it will not recognize or negotiate with the Palestine Liberation Organization so long as the Palestine Liberation Organization does not recognize Israel's right to exist and does not accept Security Council Resolutions 242 and 338."

10.   Testimony before the Subcommittee on Europe and the Middle East of the House Foreign Affairs Committee, June 24, 1992.

11.   UNSC Resolution 242 was adopted on November 22, 1967, and has become the basis for subsequent efforts to resolve the Arab-Israeli conflict. Among other elements it calls for "withdrawal of Israeli armed forces from territories occupied in the recent conflict" and for peace — thus the "territories for peace" concept.

12.   Texts of the letters are in *New York Times*, February 17, 1982.

13.   Robert M. Gates, "The Global Challenge to American Intelligence," Town Hall of California, December 15, 1992, p. 14.

14.   Les Aspin,"Session IV, Congressman Les Aspin, Chairman, House Armed Services Committee,"in *The Soref Symposium: The Middle East in an Era of Changing Superpower Relations, Washington, D.C., April 29–30, 1990*, edited by David Segal. (Washington, D.C.: The Washington Institute for Near East Policy, 1990), p. 40.

CHAPTER 4

1.   In the case of McCloskey, the pro-Israel lobby affected his fall from power, but other factors were involved. In Findley's and Percy's cases a more plausible argument may be made about the lobby.

2.   *New York Times*, September 13, 1991.

3.   *Near East Report*, April 13, 1992, p. 68.

4.   "Remarks of Israeli Prime Minister Yitzhak Rabin to the American Israel Public Affairs Committee, Washington, D.C., March 15, 1994." Text provided by Israel Information Service Gopher, Israel Foreign Ministry, Jerusalem.

5.   Charles McC Mathias, Jr., "Ethnic Groups and Foreign Policy," *Foreign Affairs* 59 (Summer 1991): 993.

6.   In a Gallup poll in September 1993, the response to the long-term trend question of "where your sympathies lie" showed a decline for Israel to 42 percent and an increase for the Palestinian Arabs to 15 percent but also a wide margin favoring Israel over the Palestinians.

CHAPTER 5

1.   Several caveats should be kept in mind in analyzing these data. First, unilateral financial assistance is qualitatively different from trade and investment flows. Second, exports and imports are added in this case to measure the value of total bilateral trade flows. Third, investment data represent the value of investment in a given year, not the change from year to year and, therefore, not exactly comparable to the aid and trade data.

2.   In 1990 Israel accounted for 37 percent of U.S. military assistance and 17 percent of U.S. economic assistance. Other significant recipients included Egypt ($2.2 billion), Turkey ($515 million), and Greece ($349 million). Together, these four countries accounted for half of all U.S. military and economic assistance in 1990.

3.   Public Law 101-302.

4.   Title VI, Public Law 102-391.

5.   German reparations from the Holocaust also helped finance this burden.

CHAPTER 6

1.   Speech by then Foreign Minister Yitzhak Shamir to the Knesset, September 8, 1982. Quoted in Bernard Reich, *The United States and Israel: Influence in the Special Relationship* (Westport, Conn.: Praeger, 1984), p. 217.

2.   Abba Eban, interview published in *The Jerusalem Post Supplement — Israel-U.S.*, July 4, 1984, p. vii.

Recommended Reading

The U.S.-Israel relationship has been the subject of extensive writing by scholars, academics, politicians, journalists, and other observers. Also, many of the participants in diplomatic and other connections between these two states have written memoirs and other works that provide interesting, although not always wholly accurate, accounts of the linkage. These are important sources and tell us a good deal about what happened, how these two states interacted, and — often — why.

This list is designed to suggest some of the books that may further elucidate the themes considered in this work. To begin, the reader is referred to two bibliographical collections that include thousands of books and articles on the subject of this study and related themes. They are:

Sanford R. Silverburg and Bernard Reich, *United States Foreign Policy and the Middle East/North Africa: A Bibliography of Twentieth-Century Research* (New York: Garland Publishing, 1990).
Sanford R. Silverburg and Bernard Reich, *U.S. Relations with the Middle East and North Africa: A Bibliography* (Metuchen, N.J.: The Scarecrow Press, 1994).

The list that follows is a select one — it contains only books and monographs written in English. The periodical literature is vast and the reader is referred to the bibliographical indexes just noted as well as to the bibliographies and notes in the works cited below for guidance to that literature. In addition to scholarly studies, it includes works that advocate

a particular approach in the relationship and those that are highly critical
of it, the latter group includes some that are of the conspiracy theory
genre. In sum they help to explicate the special relationship between the
United States and Israel.

Acheson, Dean. *Present at the Creation: My Years in the State Department* (New York:
    Norton, 1969).
Alteras, Isaac. *Eisenhower and Israel: U.S.-Israeli Relations, 1953–1960* (Gainesville:
    University Press of Florida, 1993).
Ariel, Yaakov S. *On Behalf of Israel: American Fundamentalist Attitudes Toward
    Jews, Judaism, and Zionism, 1865–1945* (Brooklyn, N.Y.: Carlson, 1991).
Bain, Kenneth Ray. *The March to Zion: United States Policy and the Founding of
    Israel* (College Station: Texas A&M University Press, 1979).
Ball, George W. and Douglas B. Ball. *The Passionate Attachment: America's
    Involvement with Israel, 1947 to the Present* (New York: W. W. Norton, 1992).
Bard, Mitchell Geoffrey. *The Water's Edge and Beyond: Defining the Limits to
    Domestic Influence on United States Middle East Policy* (New Brunswick, N.J.:
    Transaction, 1991).
Begin, Menachem. *The Revolt* (New York: Nash, 1981).
Ben-Gurion, David. *Israel: A Personal History* (New York: Funk and Wagnalls, 1971).
____. *Rebirth and Destiny of Israel* (New York: Philosophical Library, 1954).
Ben-Zvi, Abraham. *The United States and Israel: The Limits of the Special
    Relationship* (New York: Columbia University Press, 1993).
Blitzer, Wolf. *Between Washington and Jerusalem: A Reporter's Notebook* (New York:
    Oxford University Press, 1985).
Brzezinski, Zbigniew. *Power and Principle: Memoirs of the National Security Adviser,
    1977–1981* (New York: Farrar, Straus, Giroux, 1983).
Carter, Jimmy. *The Blood of Abraham* (Boston: Houghton Mifflin, 1985).
____. *Keeping Faith: Memoirs of a President* (New York: Bantam Books, 1982).
Chomsky, Noam. *The Fateful Triangle: The United States, Israel and the Palestinians*
    (Boston: South End Press, 1983).
Clifford, Clark, with Richard Holbrooke. *Counsel to the President: A Memoir* (New
    York: Random House, 1991).
Cockburn, Andrew and Leslie Cockburn. *Dangerous Liaison: The Inside Story of the
    U.S.-Israeli Covert Relationship* (New York: Harper Collins Publishers, 1991).
Cohen, Michael J. *Truman and Israel* (Berkeley: University of California Press, 1990).
Commission on U.S.-Israel Relations. *Enduring Partnership: Report of the
    Commission on U.S.-Israel Relations* (Washington, D.C.: Washington Institute
    for Near East Policy, 1993).
Dayan, Moshe. *Breakthrough: A Personal Account of the Egypt-Israel Peace
    Negotiations* (New York: Alfred A. Knopf, 1981).
____. *Story of My Life: An Autobiography* (New York: William Morrow, 1976).
Drinan, Robert F. *Honor the Promise: America's Commitment to Israel* (Garden City,
    N.Y.: Doubleday, 1977).
Eban, Abba. *An Autobiography* (New York: Random House, 1977).
Eisenhower, Dwight D. *The White House Years: Mandate For Change, 1953-1956*
    (Garden City, N.Y.: Doubleday, 1963).

____. *The White House Years: Waging Peace, 1956–1961* (Garden City, N.Y.: Doubleday, 1965).

Eytan, Walter. *The First Ten Years: A Diplomatic History of Israel* (New York: Simon and Schuster, 1958).

Feis, Herbert. *The Birth of Israel: The Tousled Diplomatic Bed* (New York: Norton, 1960).

Feuerwerger, Marvin C. *Congress and Israel: Foreign Aid Decision-making in the House of Representatives, 1969–1976* (Westport, Conn.: Greenwood, 1979).

Findley, Paul. *Deliberate Deceptions: Facing the Facts about the U.S.-Israeli Relationship* (Chicago: Lawrence Hill Books, 1993).

____. *They Dare to Speak Out: People and Institutions Confront Israel's Lobby* (Westport, Conn.: Lawrence Hill, 1985).

Finer, Herman. *Dulles Over Suez: The Theory and Practice of His Diplomacy* (Chicago: Quadrangle Books, 1964).

Fink, Reuben, ed. *America and Palestine: The Attitude of Official America and of the American People Toward the Rebuilding of Palestine as a Free and Democratic Jewish Commonwealth* (New York: American Zionist Emergency Council, 1944).

Ford, Gerald R. *A Time to Heal: The Autobiography of Gerald R. Ford* (New York: Harper & Row, 1979).

Gazit, Mordechai. *President Kennedy's Policy Toward the Arab States and Israel: Analysis and Documents* (Tel Aviv: Tel Aviv University, 1983).

Glick, Edward Bernard. *The Triangular Connection: America, Israel, and American Jews* (Boston: George Allen & Unwin, 1982).

Goldberg, David Howard. *Foreign Policy and Ethnic Interest Groups: American and Canadian Jews Lobby for Israel* (Westport, Conn.: Greenwood, 1990).

Green, Stephen. *Living by the Sword: America and Israel in the Middle East, 1968–87* (Brattleboro, Vt.: Amana Books, 1988).

____. *Taking Sides, America's Secret Relations with a Militant Israel* (New York: Morrow, 1984).

Grose, Peter. *Israel in the Mind of America* (New York: Alfred A. Knopf, 1983).

Haig, Alexander M., Jr. *Caveat: Realism, Reagan, and Foreign Policy* (New York: Macmillan, 1984).

Hersh, Seymour M. *The Samson Option: Israel's Nuclear Arsenal and American Foreign Policy* (New York: Random House, 1991).

Johnson, Lyndon Baines. *The Vantage Point: Perspectives of the Presidency, 1963–1969* (New York: Holt, Rinehart and Winston, 1971).

Kadi, Leila S. *A Survey of American-Israeli Relations* (Beirut: Palestine Research Center, 1969).

Kenen, I. L. *Israel's Defense Line: Her Friends and Foes in Washington* (Buffalo, N.Y.: Prometheus, 1981).

Kissinger, Henry. *White House Years* (Boston: Little, Brown, 1979).

____. *Years of Upheaval* (Boston: Little, Brown, 1982).

Kuniholm, Bruce Robellet. *The Palestinian Problem and United States Policy: A Guide to Issues and References* (Claremont, Calif.: Regina Books, 1986).

Mansur, Kamil. *Beyond Alliance: Israel in U.S. Foreign Policy* (New York: Columbia University Press, 1994).

McDonald, James G. *My Mission in Israel, 1948–1951* (New York: Simon and Schuster, 1951).

Medzini, Meron. *Israel's Foreign Relations: Selected Documents, 1947–1992*, 12 volumes (Jerusalem: Ministry for Foreign Affairs, 1976-1993).

Meir, Golda. *My Life* (New York: G. P. Putnam's Sons, 1975).

Melman, Yossi and Daniel Raviv. *Friends in Deed: Inside the U.S.-Israel Alliance* (New York: Hyperion, 1994).

Millis, Walter, ed. (with the collaboration of E. S. Duffield). *The Forrestal Diaries* (New York: Viking Press, 1951).

Nixon, Richard M. *RN: The Memoirs of Richard Nixon* (New York: Grosset & Dunlap, 1978).

Novik, Nimrod. *The United States and Israel: Domestic Determinants of a Changing U.S. Commitment* (Boulder: Westview, 1986).

Organski, A.F.K. *The $36 Billion Bargain: Strategy and Politics in U.S. Assistance to Israel* (New York: Columbia University Press, 1990).

Peres, Shimon. *David's Sling: The Arming of Israel* (London: Weidenfeld & Nicolson, 1970).

Pollock, David. *The Politics of Pressure: American Arms and Israeli Policy Since the Six Day War* (Westport, Conn.: Greenwood, 1982).

Puschel, Karen L. *US-Israeli Strategic Cooperation in the Post-Cold War Era: An American Perspective* (Boulder, Colo: Westview, 1993).

Quandt, William B. *Decade of Decisions: American Policy Toward the Arab-Israeli Conflict, 1967–1976* (Berkeley: University of California Press, 1977).

____. *Peace Process: American Diplomacy and the Arab-Israeli Conflict Since 1967* (Washington, D.C.: Brookings Institution, 1993).

Rabin, Yitzhak. *The Rabin Memoirs* (Boston: Little, Brown, 1979).

Rafael, Gideon. *Destination Peace: Three Decades of Israeli Foreign Policy, A Memoir* (New York: Stein and Day, 1981).

Ray, James Lee. *The Future of American-Israeli Relations: A Parting of the Ways?* (Lexington: University Press of Kentucky, 1985).

Reagan, Ronald. *An American Life* (New York: Simon and Schuster, 1990).

Reich, Bernard. *Quest for Peace: United States-Israel Relations and the Arab-Israeli Conflict* (New Brunswick, N.J.: Transaction, 1977).

____. *The United States and Israel: Influence in the Special Relationship* (Westport, Conn.: Praeger, 1984).

Rubenberg, Cheryl. *Israel and the American National Interest: A Critical Examination* (Urbana: University of Illinois Press, 1986).

Papp, Daniel S., ed. *As I Saw It* (New York: W. W. Norton, 1990).

Safran, Nadav. *From War to War: The Arab-Israeli Confrontation, 1948–1967* (Cambridge, Mass.: Harvard University Press, 1963).

____. *Israel, The Embattled Ally* (Cambridge, Mass.: Belknap Press, 1978).

____. *The United States and Israel* (Cambridge, Mass.: Harvard University Press, 1963).

Saunders, Harold H. *The Other Walls: The Arab-Israeli Peace Process in a Global Perspective*, rev. ed. (Princeton, N.J.: Princeton University Press, 1991).

Schoenbaum, David. *The United States and the State of Israel* (New York: Oxford University Press, 1993).

Sharon, Ariel (with David Chanoff). *Warrior: An Autobiography* (New York: Simon and Schuster, 1989).

Sheffer, Gabriel, ed. *Dynamics of Dependence: U.S.-Israeli Relations* (Boulder, Colo.: Westview, 1986).

Simon, Merrill. *Moshe Arens Stateman and Scientist Speaks Out* (Middle Island, N.Y.: Dean Books, 1988).

Snetsinger, John. *Truman, The Jewish Vote, and the Creation of Israel* (Stanford, Calif.: Hoover Institution Press, 1974).

Spiegel, Steven L. *The Other Arab-Israeli Conflict: Making America's Middle East Policy, From Truman to Reagan* (Chicago: University of Chicago Press, 1985).

Tamir, Avraham. *A Soldier in Search of Peace: An Inside Look at Israel's Strategy,* edited by Joan Comay. (New York: Harper & Row, 1988).

Tivnan, Edward. *The Lobby: Jewish Political Power and American Foreign Policy* (New York: Simon and Schuster, 1987).

Truman, Harry S. *Memoirs: Volume I Year of Decisions; II: Years of Trial and Hope* (Garden City, N.Y.: Doubleday, 1955–1956).

Vance, Cyrus. *Hard Choices: Critical Years in America's Foreign Policy* (New York: Simon and Schuster, 1983).

Weizman, Ezer. *The Battle for Peace* (New York: Bantam, 1981).

Weizmann, Chaim. *Trial and Error* (New York: Schocken, 1966).

Wilson, Evan M. *Decision on Palestine: How the U.S. Came to Recognize Israel* (Stanford, Calif.: Hoover Institution Press, 1979).

Index

ABOUT THE AUTHOR

BERNARD REICH, Professor of Political Science and International Affairs, George Washington University, is well known for his many books and articles dealing with Israeli politics and U.S. foreign policy. His writings include *Israeli Politics in the 1990s* (1991), *Israeli National Security Policy* (1988), *Powers of the Middle East and Israel* (1986), *The United States and Israel* (1984), and *Political Leaders of the Contemporary Middle East and North Africa: A Biographical Dictionary* (1993), all published by Greenwood Press, and many other works. He serves as a consultant on Middle Eastern affairs to a number of U.S. government agencies.

www.ingramcontent.com/pod-product-compliance
Lightning Source LLC
Chambersburg PA
CBHW062031270326
41929CB00014B/2395